First World War
and Army of Occupation
War Diary
France, Belgium and Germany

30 DIVISION
Headquarters, Branches and Services
Royal Army Ordnance Corps
Deputy Assistant Director Ordnance Services
7 November 1915 - 31 March 1919

WO95/2320/2

The Naval & Military Press Ltd
www.nmarchive.com
Published in association with The National Archives

Published by

The Naval & Military Press Ltd

Unit 10 Ridgewood Industrial Park,

Uckfield, East Sussex,

TN22 5QE England

Tel: +44 (0) 1825 749494

www.naval-military-press.com

www.nmarchive.com

This diary has been reprinted in facsimile from the original. Any imperfections are inevitably reproduced and the quality may fall short of modern type and cartographic standards.

Contents

Document type	Place/Title	Date From	Date To
Heading	Deputy Assistant Director Ordnance Services		
Heading	30th Division Divl Troops Asst Dir. Vety Services Nov 1915- Mar 1919		
Heading	H.Q. 30th Div. A.D.R.S. Vol I Nov 15		
War Diary	Solitary Plan	07/11/1915	07/11/1915
War Diary	Boulogne	07/11/1915	07/11/1915
War Diary	Ailly-Le-Haut Clocher	08/11/1915	11/11/1915
Heading	Volume 1 A D V S 30th Division		
War Diary	Ailly Le Haut Clocher	11/11/1915	17/11/1915
War Diary	Mascelles	18/11/1915	27/11/1915
War Diary	Fienvillers	28/11/1915	30/11/1915
Heading	A.D.V.S. 30th Div. Vol 2 121/7910		
War Diary	Fienvillers	01/12/1915	04/12/1915
War Diary	Le Milliard	05/12/1915	07/12/1915
Heading	Volume 2 H.C. Welch Maj. A.V.C. A.D.V.S. 30th Div 1.1.16		
War Diary	Le Milliard	07/12/1915	31/12/1915
Heading	30th Div. A.D.V.S 30th Div. Vol 3 Jan 16		
War Diary	Le Milliard	01/01/1916	07/01/1916
War Diary	Daours	08/01/1916	09/01/1916
Heading	Volume 3-1916 H.C. Welch Major AVC A.D.V.S 30th Division		
War Diary	Daours	09/01/1916	11/01/1916
War Diary	Etinehem	12/01/1916	09/02/1916
Heading	Volume Feb 29 1916 H.C. Welch Major A.D.V.S 30th Div.		
War Diary	Etinehem	10/02/1916	25/02/1916
Heading	ADVS 30th Div Vol 5		
War Diary	Etinehem	12/03/1916	20/03/1916
Heading	Volume 5 March 31.3.16 H.C. Welch Major ADVS 30th Div		
War Diary	Etinehem	20/03/1916	20/03/1916
War Diary	Daours	21/03/1916	27/03/1916
War Diary	Ailly-Sur-Somme	28/03/1916	10/04/1916
Heading	Volume 6 April 30 1916 H.C. Welch Maj ADVS 30th Division		
War Diary	Ailly. Sur. Somme	11/04/1916	30/05/1916
War Diary	Etinehem	06/05/1916	10/05/1916
Heading	Volume 7 May 31.16 H.C. Welch Major		
War Diary	Etinehem	11/05/1916	13/06/1916
Heading	Volume 8 H.C. Welch Maj ADVS 30th Div June 30. 1916		
War Diary	Etinehem	14/06/1916	05/07/1916
Heading	Volume 9. Ending July 31 1916 H.C. Welch Major ADVS 30th Division		
War Diary	Etinehem	06/07/1916	14/07/1916
War Diary	Corbie	15/07/1916	22/07/1916
War Diary	Battle Dugouts L.16.b.55	23/07/1916	25/07/1916
War Diary	Battle Dugouts	25/07/1916	26/07/1916
War Diary	Bay Albert Rd F.26.d.1.1	27/07/1916	30/07/1916

War Diary	Bay Albert Rd	31/07/1916	31/07/1916
Heading	War Diary of the A.D.V.S. 30th Division for the month of August 1916 Volume 10 ADVS Vol 10		
War Diary	Bray Albert Rd F.26.d. 1.1	01/08/1916	01/08/1916
War Diary	Hallencourt	02/08/1916	04/08/1916
War Diary	Busnes	05/08/1916	07/08/1916
Heading	Volume 10 Ending Aug 31-1916 H.C. Welch Maj ADVS 30th Division		
War Diary	Busnes	07/08/1916	12/08/1916
War Diary	Bethune	13/08/1916	31/08/1916
Heading	War Diary of A.D.V.S, 30th Division for the month of September 1916 Volume XI H.C. Welch Major		
War Diary	Bethune	01/09/1916	09/09/1916
Heading	Volume 11. Ending September 30/1916 H.C. Welch Major ADVS 30th Div		
War Diary	Bethune	09/09/1916	18/09/1916
War Diary	Doullens	19/09/1916	21/09/1916
War Diary	Vignacourt	22/09/1916	30/09/1916
Heading	War Diary of A.D.V.S. 30th Division for the Month of October 1916 Volume 12 H.C. Welch Major		
War Diary	Vignacourt	01/10/1916	04/10/1916
War Diary	Buire	05/10/1916	08/10/1916
Heading	Volume 12 Ending October 31-1916 H.C. Welch Major ADVS 30th Division		
War Diary	Buire	09/10/1916	11/10/1916
War Diary	E 11 Central	12/10/1916	17/10/1916
War Diary	Fricourt Chateau	18/10/1916	22/10/1916
War Diary	Ribemont	23/10/1916	26/10/1916
War Diary	Pas	27/10/1916	30/10/1916
War Diary	Bavincourt	31/10/1916	31/10/1916
Heading	War Diary of A.D.V.S. 30th Divn for the month of November 1916 Volume XIII		
War Diary	Bavincourt	01/11/1916	05/11/1916
Heading	Volume 13 Ending November 30 1916 H.C. Welch Major ADVS 30th Division		
War Diary	Bavincourt	06/11/1916	30/11/1916
Heading	War Diary of A.D.V.S, 30th Division. for the month of December 1916 Volume 14		
War Diary	Bavincourt	01/12/1916	06/12/1916
Heading	Volume 14 H.C. Welch Maj. ADVS 30th Division Month Ending December 1916		
War Diary	Bavincourt	06/12/1916	31/12/1916
Heading	War Diary of A.D.V.S. 30th Division for the month of January 1917 Volume 15		
War Diary	Bavincourt	01/01/1917	12/01/1917
War Diary	Lucheux	13/01/1917	31/01/1917
Heading	War Diary of A.D.V.S. 30th Division for the Month of February 1917		
War Diary	Lucheux	05/02/1917	06/02/1917
War Diary	Berneville	07/02/1917	28/02/1917
Heading	War Diary of A.D.V.S. 30th Div for the month of March 1917 Volume 17		
War Diary	Berneville	01/03/1917	23/03/1917
War Diary	Bretencourt	24/03/1917	31/03/1917
Heading	War Diary of A.D.V.S. 30th Div. for the month of April 1917		

War Diary	Bretencourt	01/04/1917	12/04/1917
War Diary	Pommier	13/04/1917	18/04/1917
War Diary	Achicourt	19/04/1917	29/04/1917
War Diary	Roellecourt	30/04/1917	30/04/1917
Heading	R.A. Gooderidge Major AVC A.D.V.S 30th Div.		
Heading	War Diary of A.D.V.S. 30th Divn. for the Month of May 1917 Volume 1917		
War Diary	Roellecourt	01/05/1917	03/05/1917
War Diary	Oeuf	04/05/1917	14/05/1917
War Diary	Willeman	15/05/1917	20/05/1917
War Diary	Pernes	21/05/1917	21/05/1917
War Diary	Norrent Fontes	22/05/1917	24/05/1917
War Diary	Steenbecque	25/05/1917	25/05/1917
War Diary	Caestre	26/05/1917	26/05/1917
War Diary	Watou	27/05/1917	30/05/1917
War Diary	Brandhoek	31/05/1917	31/05/1917
Heading	R.A. Gooderidge Major AVC ADVS 30th Div.		
Heading	War Diary of D.A.D.V.S. 30th Div. for the month of June 1917 Volume XX		
War Diary	Brandhoek H 7 C 88	01/06/1917	10/06/1917
War Diary	Brandhoek	11/06/1917	13/06/1917
War Diary	Reninghelst	14/06/1917	30/06/1917
Heading	War Diary of D.A.D.V.S. 30th Div. for the month of July 1917 Vol 21		
War Diary	Reninghelst	01/07/1917	07/07/1917
War Diary	Nordausques	08/07/1917	19/07/1917
War Diary	Steenvoorde	20/07/1917	24/07/1917
War Diary	Reninghelst	25/07/1917	31/07/1917
Heading	War Diary for month of August 1917 D.A.D.V.S. 30th Divn Vol XXII Vol 22		
War Diary	Reninghelst	01/08/1917	05/08/1917
War Diary	Godewaersvelde	06/08/1917	07/08/1917
War Diary	Merris	08/08/1917	11/08/1917
War Diary	St Jans Cappel	12/08/1917	23/08/1917
War Diary	Dranoutre	24/08/1917	31/08/1917
Heading	War Diary of D.A.D.V.S. 30th Divn. for the month of September 1917 Volume XXIII		
War Diary	Dranoutre	01/09/1917	30/09/1917
Heading	War Diary of D.A.D.V.S. 30th Divn. for the month of October 1917 Volume 24		
War Diary	Dranoutre	01/10/1917	31/10/1917
Heading	War Diary of D.A.D.V.S. 30th Divn. for the month of November 1917 Volume XXV		
War Diary	Dranoutre	01/11/1917	15/11/1917
War Diary	Steenvoorde	16/11/1917	27/11/1917
War Diary	Westoutre	28/11/1917	30/11/1917
Heading	War Diary of D.A.D.V.S. 30th Divn. for the month of December 1917 Volume XXVI		
War Diary	Westoutre	01/12/1917	31/12/1917
Heading	D.A.D.V.S		
Heading	War Diary of D.A.D.V.S. 30th Divn. for the month of January 1918 Vol XXVII		
War Diary	Westoutre	01/01/1918	06/01/1918
War Diary	Blaringhem	07/01/1918	09/01/1918
War Diary	Corbie	10/01/1918	14/01/1918
War Diary	Nesle	15/01/1918	19/01/1918

War Diary	Ercheu	20/01/1918	28/01/1918
War Diary	Chauny	29/01/1918	31/01/1918
Heading	War Diary of D.A.D.V.S. 30th Divn. for the month of February 1918 Volume XXVIII		
War Diary	Chauny	01/02/1918	02/02/1918
War Diary	Villequier-Aumont	03/02/1918	09/02/1918
War Diary	Ercheu	10/02/1918	22/02/1918
War Diary	Ham	23/02/1918	26/02/1918
War Diary	Dury	27/02/1918	28/02/1918
Heading	War Diary of D.A.D.V.S. 30th Divn. for the month of March 1918 Volume XXIX		
War Diary	Dury	01/03/1918	21/03/1918
War Diary	Ercheu	22/03/1918	23/03/1918
War Diary	Roiglise	24/03/1918	26/03/1918
War Diary	Hangest En Santerre	26/03/1918	26/03/1918
War Diary	Braches	26/03/1918	26/03/1918
War Diary	Ailly Sur Noye	26/03/1918	26/03/1918
War Diary	Estrees Sur Noye	29/03/1918	30/03/1918
War Diary	St Valery Sur Somme	31/03/1918	31/03/1918
Heading	War Diary for the Month of April 1918 of D.A.D.V.S. 30th Division Volume XXX		
War Diary	St. Valery Sur Somme	01/04/1918	05/04/1918
War Diary	Proven	06/04/1918	08/04/1918
War Diary	Canal Bank Ypres	09/04/1918	11/04/1918
War Diary	Elverdinghe	12/04/1918	13/04/1918
War Diary	St. Sixte	14/04/1918	20/04/1918
War Diary	Catterick-Camp	21/04/1918	26/04/1918
War Diary	Broxeele	27/04/1918	30/04/1918
Heading	War Diary of D.A.D.V.S. 30th. Division for the Month of May 1918 Volume XXXI		
War Diary	Broxeele	01/05/1918	14/05/1918
War Diary	Broxeele	15/05/1918	15/05/1918
War Diary	Eu	16/05/1918	31/05/1918
Heading	War Diary of D.A.D.V.S. 30th Divn. for the month of June 1918 Volume XXXII		
War Diary	Eu	01/06/1918	20/06/1918
War Diary	Rue	21/06/1918	27/06/1918
War Diary	Eperleques	28/06/1918	30/06/1918
Heading	War Diary of D.A.D.V.S. 30th Divn. for July 1918 Volume XXXIII		
War Diary	Eperlecques	01/07/1918	14/07/1918
War Diary	Cassel	15/07/1918	31/07/1918
Heading	War Diary of D.A.D.V.S. 30th British Division for the month of August 1918		
War Diary	Terdeghem	01/08/1918	10/08/1918
War Diary	Cassel	10/08/1918	10/08/1918
War Diary	Terdeghem	11/08/1918	31/08/1918
Heading	War Diary. September 1918 Vol XXXV. D.A.D.V.S. 30th British Division.		
War Diary	La. Montagne	01/09/1918	30/09/1918
Heading	War Diary of D.A.D.V.S. 30th Divn. for month of October 1918		
War Diary	Mount Noir	01/10/1918	01/10/1918
War Diary	Dranoutre	02/10/1918	17/10/1918
War Diary	Kortewilde	18/10/1918	19/10/1918
War Diary	Roncq	20/10/1918	21/10/1918

War Diary	Aelbeke	22/10/1918	31/10/1918
Heading	War Diary of D.A.D.V.S. 30th Division for month of November 1918 Volume XXXVII		
War Diary	Aelbeke	01/11/1918	12/11/1918
War Diary	Renaix	13/11/1918	15/11/1918
War Diary	Mouscron	16/11/1918	30/11/1918
Heading	War Diary of D.A.D.V.S. 30th Division for December 1918 Volume XXXVIII		
War Diary	Mouscron	01/12/1918	02/12/1918
War Diary	Renescure	03/12/1918	31/12/1918
Heading	War Diary of D.A.D.V.S. 30th Division for month of January 1919 Volume XXXIX		
War Diary	Remescure	01/01/1919	13/01/1919
War Diary	La Capelle	14/01/1919	31/01/1919
Heading	War Diary of D.A.D.V.S. 30th Division for February 1919 Volume XL		
War Diary	La Capelle	01/02/1919	25/02/1919
War Diary	Condette	26/02/1919	28/02/1919
Heading	War Diary of D.A.D.V.S. 30th Divn. for month of March 1919 Volume XLI		
War Diary	Condette	01/03/1919	31/03/1919

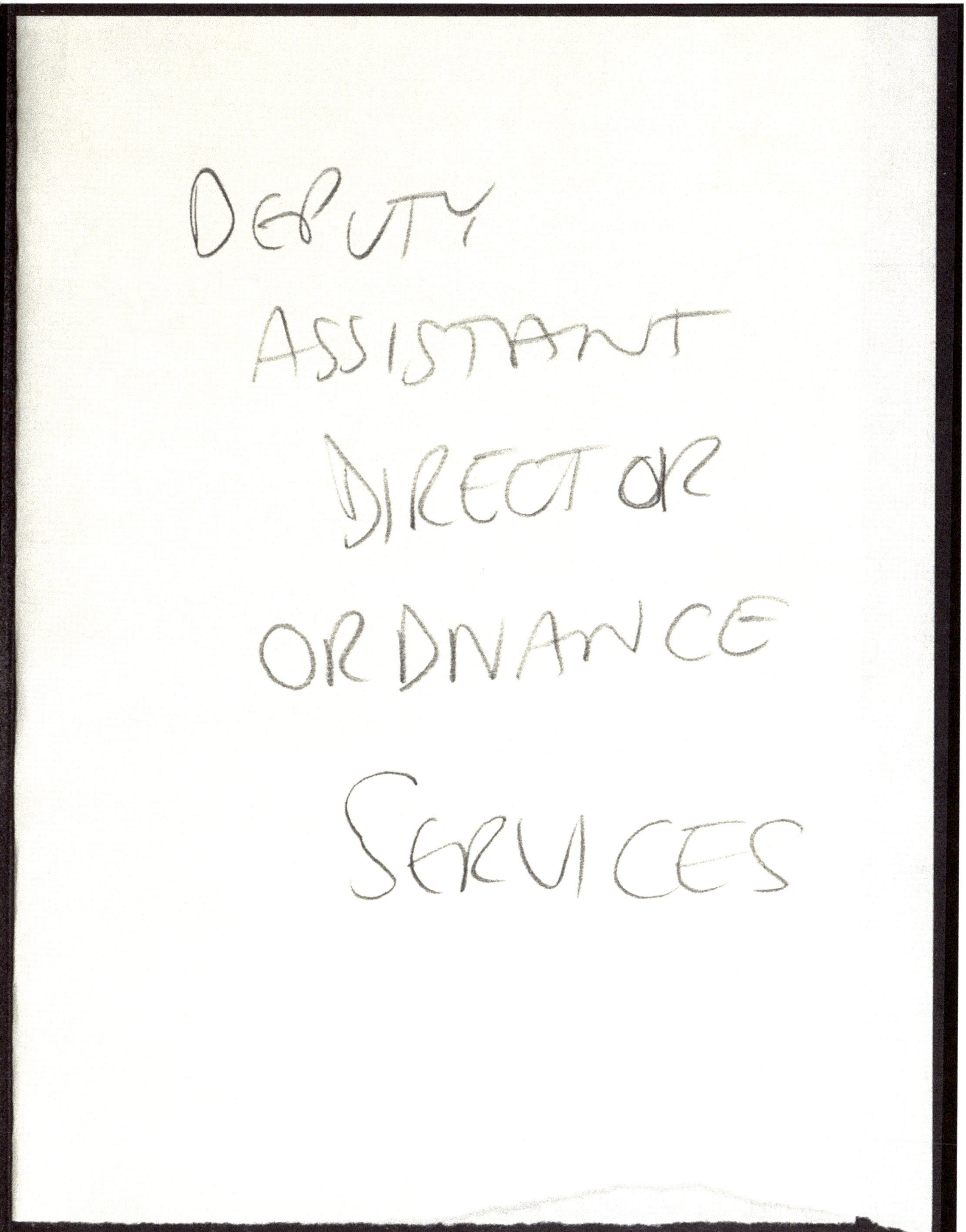
DEPUTY
ASSISTANT
DIRECTOR
ORDINANCE
SERVICES

30TH DIVISION
DIVL TROOPS

ASST DIR. VETY SERVICES
NOV 1915-MAR 1919

H.Q. 30th Div: A.D.M.S.
Vol I

121
7708

S

Nov 15

Instructions regarding War Diaries and Intelligence Summaries are contained in F. S. Regs., Part II. and the Staff Manual respectively. Title pages will be prepared in manuscript.

WAR DIARY
or
INTELLIGENCE SUMMARY. A.D.V.S 30th Division

(*Erase heading not required.*)

Army Form C. 2118.

Place	Date	Hour	Summary of Events and Information	Remarks and references to Appendices
Salisbury Plain	7 11/15	7.30 a.m.	Left Larkhill Camp, Salisbury Plain. Entrained with Head Quarters 30th Division at Amesbury Station. Train left at 8.40 a.m. Arrived at Folkestone 2 P.m. Embarked at 2.15 P.m. Left Folkestone harbour at 2.50 P.m. arrived Boulogne at 6 P.m. disembarked at 6.30 P.m.	
Boulogne	7. 11/15		Billeted this night at Hotel du Louvre. ~~Left Boulogne~~	
Ailly-le-haut Clocher	8 11/15		Left Boulogne by car for Ailly le Haut Clocher arrived 1.30 P.m. Reported to D.V.S. Abbeville.	
"	9 11/15		Lieut Clawson A.V.C. V.O. to 22nd Divisional Train reported himself. Visited Head Quarters 89th Infantry Bde. also the 17th 18th 19th and 20th Liverpool Regiments. Inspected the horses of Divisional Train.	
"	10 11/15		Visited Head Quarters 90th Infantry Bde at St Riquier. Interviewed Lieut Clapp A.V.C. Called on the D.V.S. Head Quarters I.G.C. Abbeville.	
"	11 11/15		Lieut Williamson A.V.C. Officer Commanding No 40 Mobile Veterinary Section arrived at Ailly le haut Clocher. Visited the 97th Field Ambulance at Bettencourt. Visited 21st Manchester Battalion inspected transport animals. Had the following put in Divisional Orders - Should the services of a Veterinary Officer be	

2353 Wt. W2544/1454 700,000 5/15 D. D. & L. A.D.S.S. Forms/C 2118.

Volume 1.

ADV.S. 30th Division

Army Form C. 2118.

Instructions regarding War Diaries and Intelligence Summaries are contained in F. S. Regs., Part II. and the Staff Manual respectively. Title pages will be prepared in manuscript.

WAR DIARY
or
INTELLIGENCE SUMMARY.
(Erase heading not required.)

Place	Date	Hour	Summary of Events and Information	Remarks and references to Appendices
Ailly le haut Clocher	11/4/15		be required by units concerned - application should be made to the nearest at Hallencourt - St Riquier or Ailly le - haut Clocher.	
" "	12/4/15		Visited Bettencourt inspected the animals of 202. Field Co R.E. - Inspected transport animals of 24th Manchester Battalion - Visited [illegible] Train sick lines	
" "	13/4/15		Visited Head Quarters 91st Infantry Bde at Gorenflos - also inspected the transport animals of the Bde at Mouflers - Vauchelles - Bucamps and Yaucourt - also visited 11th Pioneer Battalion South Lancs at Bussus and Head Quarters 90th Infantry Bde at St Riquier	
" "	14/4/15		Visited 149 Army Troops Company R.E. at Vignacourt - and No 1. Section Auxiliary horse transport at Argoeuves.	
" "	15/4/15		Short day at Head Quarters in Office. Wrote instructions through Divisional orders re frost bite in [illegible] -	
" "	16/4/15		Inspected No 40. Mobile Veterinary Section.	
" "	17/4/15	8.30 AM	Left Ailly le haut Clocher with Head Quarters for Hallencourt - arrived Hallencourt by motor car at 10 am - Inspected animals of 24th Manchester Battalion and 11th South Lancs at Hallencourt - Interviewed with a billet or office	
Hallencourt	18/4/15		No 40 Mobile Veterinary Section arrived at Hallencourt - Billets and accommodation for sick animals bad -	
	19/4/15		Visited 90th Infantry Bde at Montor Villiers - Villiers Bocage - Bertangles Cardonette and Poix -	
	20/4/15		Visited 202 Field Co R.E. at Villiers Bocage 24th Manchester Battalion at [illegible] and 97th Field Ambulance at [illegible] -	

2353 Wt. W2544/1454 700,000 5/15 D. D. & L. A.D.S.S. Forms/C 2118.

Instructions regarding War Diaries and Intelligence Summaries are contained in F. S. Regs., Part II. and the Staff Manual respectively. Title pages will be prepared in manuscript.

Army Form C. 2118.

WAR DIARY
or
INTELLIGENCE SUMMARY.
(Erase heading not required.)

Place	Date	Hour	Summary of Events and Information	Remarks and references to Appendices
Hascelles	21/11/15		Visited D Squadron Lancashire Hussars at Olincourt - No 1 Section Auxiliary Horse Transport at Argoeuves - Proceeded to Amiens to try and arrange for a Horse Ambulance to collect horses left behind by the 26th Division - Great inconvenience is caused by not having an ambulance with Mobile Veterinary Section. Recommend the most [illegible], and a motor ambulance large enough to carry two horses at a time for preference	
"	22/11/15		Visited No 40 Mobile Veterinary Section - also 91st Infantry Bde	
"	23/11/15		At Head quarters -	
"	24/11/15		Visited Olincourt - Airaincourt - St Vast - Coisy and Vaours inspecting sick horses for evacuation - All these horses were ambulance cases and great difficulty was experienced in obtaining a horse ambulance to remove them - thus I eventually arranged at Amiens and took them to Railhead	
"	25/11/15		Visited 149 Army Troops Co R.E. at Vignacourt	
"	26/11/15		" " " " Inspected No 40 Mobile Veterinary Section.	
"	27/11/15		At Head Quarters	
Frenvillers	28/11/15		Left Hescelles at 8.30 am with Head Quarters - for Frenvillers arrived 10.30 am Head Quarters of Division went to Le Mesnil - The remainder at Frenvillers - No 40 Mobile Veterinary Section moved to Vacquerie - very good billets and accommodation for sick animals	

2353 Wt. W2544/1454 700,000 5/15 D. D. & L. A.D.S.S. Forms/C. 2118.

Army Form C. 21[?]

WAR DIARY
or
INTELLIGENCE SUMMARY.
(Erase heading not required.)

Instructions regarding War Diaries and Intelligence Summaries are contained in F. S. Regs., Part II. and the Staff Manual respectively. Title pages will be prepared in manuscript.

Place	Date	Hour	Summary of Events and Information	Remarks and references to Appendices
Fienvillers	29/11/15		At Fienvillers. No car available to visit units	
" "	30/11/15		Visited Mobile Veterinary Section at Vacquerie - 96th Field Ambulance at Bertaucourt - 90th Infantry Bde at Canaples - Inspected 97th Field Ambulance at Fienvillers.	
			The following Veterinary officers are doing duty with this Division	
			Lieut McIver (H.P.) AVC embarked November 6th at Southampton with 89th Infantry Bde	
			Lieut Clapp (A.H.) AVC " " " 7th " " " " 90th " "	
			Lieut Williamson (D.R.) AVC " " " " 9th " " " " No 40 Mobile V. Section	
			Lieut Clunes (F.L.) AVC reported himself for duty with Divisional Train November 9th	
			Lieut Keslen (S.H.) AVC embarked November 29th at Southampton with 150th Bde R.F.A.	
			Lieut Adams (F.J.) AVC " " " " 28th " " " " 148 Bde R.F.A.	
			H. C. Welch Major ADVS 30th Division	

Army Form C. 2118.

Instructions regarding War Diaries and Intelligence Summaries are contained in F. S. Regs., Part II. and the Staff Manual respectively. Title pages will be prepared in manuscript.

WAR DIARY
or
INTELLIGENCE SUMMARY.
(Erase heading not required.)

Place	Date	Hour	Summary of Events and Information	Remarks and references to Appendices
Frevillers	Dec 1st		Visited No 40 Mobile Veterinary Section at Vacquerie	
"	" 2		At Frevillers	
"	" 3		Visited Head Quarters 149 Bde R.F.A at Pernois – 150th at Berlancourt 148 at St Leger 151st at St Ouen and Divisional Head Quarters Artillery at St Ouen	
"	" 4		At Frevillers	
			Visited Mobile Veterinary Section at Vacquerie	
Le Meillard	5		Moved from Frevillers at 9 30 am – to join Head Quarters of the Division at Le Meillard – arrived 10 am.	
"	6		Visited Berlancourt inspected horses 150th Bde R.F.A.	
			Inspected farm yard of Emile Alexandre La Place Bernaville had some out of bounds – it is believed 1/2 London Bde R.F.A occupied these premises as sick lines and informed A.D.V.S a case of Glanders had been confirmed in one of the horses stabled at Ruspel Fermence – Route de Domart – Bernaville which latter place I also visited and had put out of bounds.	
" "	7th		Visited Head Qrs 91st Infantry Bde at Frevillers, several horses had wounds on [illegible]	

2353 Wt. W2544/1454 700,000 5/15 D. D. & L. A.D.S.S. Forms/C. 2118.

Volume 2.

H Welch Maj AVC

ADVS 30th Div

1. 1. 16

Instructions regarding War Diaries and Intelligence Summaries are contained in F. S. Regs., Part II. and the Staff Manual respectively. Title pages will be prepared in manuscript.

WAR DIARY
or
INTELLIGENCE SUMMARY.
(Erase heading not required.)

Army Form C. 2118.

Place	Date	Hour	Summary of Events and Information	Remarks and references to Appendices
Le Meillard ~~[illegible]~~	9th		of the horses thru necks, due to carrying nose bags - Visited Canaples inspected transport animals 22nd Manchesters.	
" "	8		Inspected Mobile V Section at Vacquerie.	
" "	9		Visited Hd Qrs Co A.S.C. Bernaville - No 2 Company Bernaville - No 3 Company Hiermont.	
" "	10th		Visited 151st Bde R.F.A and Divisional Ammunition column at St Ouen - in these units there were a number of neck wounds from carrying nose bags - Had attention drawn to it through divisional orders.	
"	11		Visited Mobile V. Section at Vacquerie & 149 Bde R.F.A Pernois	
"	12		Visited 150th Bde at Bertancourt re deaths amongst the horses from Pneumonia.	
"	13		Visited 21st Manchester Battalion at Flesselles - also the 22nd at Canaples - Several cases of debility in the former unit - the shoeing in some instances was bad - Called at Head Quarters of the Bde 91st drawing attention to the matter.	

2353 Wt. W2544/1454 700,000 5/15 D. D. & L. A.D.S.S. Forms/C 2118.

Instructions regarding War Diaries and Intelligence Summaries are contained in F. S. Regs., Part II. and the Staff Manual respectively. Title pages will be prepared in manuscript.

WAR DIARY
or
INTELLIGENCE SUMMARY.
(Erase heading not required.)

Army Form C. 2118.

Place	Date	Hour	Summary of Events and Information	Remarks and references to Appendices
St [illegible] ~~[illegible]~~	Dec 14th		Visited 96 Field Ambulance at St Leger. V.O. i/c St Kesten reported four cases in this unit suspicious of mange - found no mange in unit whatever.	
" "	15th		Inspected 148, 149 & 150 Bde R.F.A. In the 149 Bde B Battery there were some 10 animals in poor condition also a similar number in the Bde Ammunition Column. Sent report to Hd Qrs Division on the matter.	
" "	16		Visited Mobile V Section - also inspected 201 Coy R.E. at Courcelles	
	17		In Office at Head Quarters.	
" "	18		Visited Divisional Ammunition Column and 151st Bde R.F.A. Met D.D. of V.S. (St Colonel Ance) 3rd Army. Many of the horses of D.A.C. without nose bags and feeding off the ground losing about 1/3 of their food. Officer Commanding D.A.C. also reports shortage of hay ration - also a large quantity of maize supplied in place of Oats - Inspected Military Mounted Police at Divisional Head Quarters	

Army Form C. 2118.

WAR DIARY
or
INTELLIGENCE SUMMARY.
(Erase heading not required.)

Instructions regarding War Diaries and Intelligence Summaries are contained in F. S. Regs., Part II. and the Staff Manual respectively. Title pages will be prepared in manuscript.

Place	Date	Hour	Summary of Events and Information	Remarks and references to Appendices
Le Mellieux	Dec 19		Inspected 98 Field Ambulance at Vacquerie	
"	20th		Visited Mobile Veterinary Section " " " and 2nd Yorks at Frenillers	
			Inspected horses of the Head Qrs Staff 30th Division	
"	21		At Le Mellieux - Applied for a car to visit artillery area - no car available	
"	22		Inspected Transport animals 2nd [illegible] at Athens some of the animals on the [illegible] - Went on to Frenillers and inspected Transport animals of the 2nd Yorks - had one horse sent to Mobile Veterinary Section for Sarcoptic mange - These Regiments have recently joined the Division	
"	23rd		Visited Mobile Veterinary Section Vacquerie	
			Inspected animals of Head Qrs Divisional Signalling Co	
"	24		Inspected 148 Bde at St. Leger - also 2nd Royal Scot Fusiliers at Canaples -	
"			Called on Senior Supply Officer of the Division re shortage of hay ration to some units of artillery and reserve of forage issued	
"	25		Xmas day - In office	
"	26		Visited 149 Bde R F A	
"	27		Inspected No 40 Mobile V. Section	

Army Form C. 2118.

Instructions regarding War Diaries and Intelligence Summaries are contained in F. S. Regs., Part II. and the Staff Manual respectively. Title pages will be prepared in manuscript.

WAR DIARY
or
INTELLIGENCE SUMMARY.
(Erase heading not required.)

Place	Date	Hour	Summary of Events and Information	Remarks and references to Appendices
Le Meillard	Dec 28		Inspected transport animals 2nd Bedfordshire Regiment at Ribeaucourt – 16th Manchester Bn at Bonneville – 11th South Lancs at Canaples	
	29th		Malleining horses Head Quarters Staff at Vacquerie	
			Visited Fienvillers with G. O. C. and inspected transport of the 30th Divisional Train	
	31		Visited Pernois and met the following Veterinary Officers Lieuts Clapp, McIntire, Rosteraud and Adam – instructed them in the palpebral method of malleinisation.	
			H C Webb Maj ADVS 30th Div 1. 1. 16	

30th Div.

A.D.M.S. 30th Div.

Vol: 3

Jan '16

Instructions regarding War Diaries and Intelligence Summaries are contained in F. S. Regs., Part II. and the Staff Manual respectively. Title pages will be prepared in manuscript.

WAR DIARY
or
INTELLIGENCE SUMMARY.
(Erase heading not required.)

Army Form C. 2118.

Place	Date	Hour	Summary of Events and Information	Remarks and references to Appendices
Le Meillard				
January 1st	1916		Visited 150 Bde R F A Bertancourt	
Le Meillard	Jan 2nd		Visited No 40. Mobile Veterinary Section Vacquerie	
			Inspected Divisional Head Qrs Signalling Co animals – Some on the forside screw. C.O's attention to this	
" "	3rd		Inspected Lancashire Hussars at Vacquerie – Issued circulars to V.O's on cracked Heels.	
" "	~~4~~		Had [?] inserted in Divisional Orders also.	
" "	4th		Visited 149 Bde Prouville and 150th Bertancourt inspecting horses of these Bdes that had been tested with mallein. Saw one horse of the 150th Bde doubtful reactor. Visited 148 Bde R F A St Leger reference mallein test. Visited the V. Section Vacquerie	
" "	5th		Visited No 40 Mobile V Section to inspect 2 suspected cases of mange.	
" "	6		Visited 150th Bde R.F.A. Bertancourt saw 2 horses of the Ammunition Column – doubtful reactors to the mallein test – had them sent to Mobile V. Section – also the one seen previously of B Battery of this Bde	
	7th		At Head Qrs Le Meillard	
DAOURS	8th		Left Le Meillard with Head Quarters of Division for ~~Le Meillard~~ DAOURS.	
	9th		Visited [illegible] to see ADVS 5th Division re his office – for the purpose of taking it over when the 30th Division come into this area on January 12th	

Volume 3 - 1916

H Church [illegible]

ADVS. 30th Division

Instructions regarding War Diaries and Intelligence Summaries are contained in F. S. Regs., Part II. and the Staff Manual respectively. Title pages will be prepared in manuscript.

WAR DIARY
or
INTELLIGENCE SUMMARY.
(Erase heading not required.)

Army Form C. 2118.

Place	Date	Hour	Summary of Events and Information	Remarks and references to Appendices
DAOURS	Jan 9th		Visited Vet. Units DAOURS probability of [illegible] to [illegible] [illegible] out of bounds – owing to a case of mange in a horse (civilian) probability of [illegible].	
	10		At Head Qrs	
	11		At Head Qrs	
[illegible]	12		Left DAOURS at 12.30 P.M. for Etinehem (?) arrived Etinehem (?) 2 P.M.	
	13		At Head Qrs	
	14		Visited Lancashire Hussars at Chipilly – also 12th & 17th Batteries R.G.A. Ammunition Column on the Chipilly Rd.	
	15		Visited Bray inspected 200 Field Co R.E. – found the animals on the horselines clean [illegible] – Inspected 202 Field Co R.E. – 19th Liverpools – 2nd Yorks and 19th Manchesters	
	16		Inspected R. Battery (in Bois de Tailles) 150th Bde R.F.A. animals.	
	17		Visited Chipilly inspected Divisional Ammunition Column	
"	18		Visited Bray inspected 16th Manchesters – 1st Norfolks and 1st Cheshires and A Battery R.H.A. at Bray – also 12th Battery R.G.A. found 4 suspicious cases of skin disease in this unit, had same isolated – Visited 19th Bde R.G.A. horse lines	

Instructions regarding War Diaries and Intelligence Summaries are contained in F. S. Regs., Part II. and the Staff Manual respectively. Title pages will be prepared in manuscript.

WAR DIARY
or
INTELLIGENCE SUMMARY.
(Erase heading not required.)

Army Form C. 2118.

Place	Date	Hour	Summary of Events and Information	Remarks and references to Appendices
Etinehem				
[illegible]	Jan 18th		Wrote S.S.O. 30th Division on the subject of hay – all animals of this Division have cut down to 6 lbs	
	19th		Inspected A Battery R.F.A. of 150th Bde at Chipilly – Called on C.R.E. Chipilly	
	20		Wrote DDVS 3rd Army on the reduced hay ration of this Division – suggesting that chopped straw be supplied – especially for heavy draught animals	
			Visited Bray inspected 1st Bedfordshire Regiment & 1st Cheshire Regiment	
			Inspected 11th South Lancs at Froissy	
	21		Visited Morlancourt inspected No 1 Coy A.S.C. 30th Divisional Train	
			Inspected No 2 Section of 14th Reserve Park	
			Sergeant Beaumont A.V.C. reported for duty with 151st Bde R.F.A.	
			Sergt Shannon A.V.C. reported himself from leave. No 40 Mobile V. Section arrived Chipilly	
	22		Captain Williamson A.V.C. O.C. No 40 Mob. V. Section reported no accommodation in Chipilly for section – went to Hd Qrs arranged for accommodation in Etinehem accommodation [illegible] Section arrived 5-30 P.m.	

Instructions regarding War Diaries and Intelligence Summaries are contained in F. S. Regs., Part II. and the Staff Manual respectively. Title pages will be prepared in manuscript.

WAR DIARY
or
INTELLIGENCE SUMMARY.
(Erase heading not required.)

Army Form C. 2118.

Place	Date	Hour	Summary of Events and Information	Remarks and references to Appendices
Etinehem	Jan 23		Endeavouring to obtain more stabling for No 40 Mobile V. Section	
			Wrote SSO 30th Division about the small quantity of hay issued to the horses of this Division asking if hay could not be purchased locally to make up the deficiency –	
"	24		Inspected Ammunition Column 148 Bde R.F.A. these horses are on the light side – some being in distinctly poor condition – also inspected D Battery same Bde & C former looking very well latter fair	
"	25		Inspected 149 Bde R.F.A. at Suzanne Wood generally condition of animals fair some very poor animals in the Ammunition Column – Inspected in the same area 17th Bn Liverpools – 19th Manchesters – 201st Co. R.E. & 16th Manchesters – latter in fair condition	
"	26th		Inspected A & B Batteries 150th Bde at Bray also C Battery and Ammunition Column Bois de Tailles – looking well	
"	27		Inspected Divisional Ammunition Column and Indian Cavalry section of D.A.C at Chipilly – No 13899 Pte G. A Willett A.V.C reported himself for duty as clerk in this office	
"	28		Inspected 2. 3 and 4 Companies A.S.C 30th Divisional Train at Etinehem.	
			Issued circular memos to all V.O's on Mange. Laminitis and debilitated horses – also on Mobile V Section stating that it is not a dumping ground for every sick animal – that certain cases should be treated in the Regimental sick lines	

2353 Wt. W2544/1454 700,000 5/15 D. D. & L. A.D.S.S. Forms/C. 2118.

WAR DIARY
or
INTELLIGENCE SUMMARY.
(Erase heading not required.)

Army Form C. 2118.

Instructions regarding War Diaries and Intelligence Summaries are contained in F. S. Regs., Part II. and the Staff Manual respectively. Title pages will be prepared in manuscript.

Place	Date	Hour	Summary of Events and Information	Remarks and references to Appendices
Etinhem	Jan 29		Inspected C. Battery 151st Bde R.F.A. on the Chilly Rd a dozen horses in very poor condition. – Inspected A Battery same Bde at Bray.	
.. ..	30		Inspecting horses in No 40. Mobile V Section.	
.. ..	31		Inspected B Battery 149 Bde R.F.A. and D Battery 150 Bde in Bois de Tailles. Had an order inserted in Divisional Routine orders re the number of horses lamed from picking up nails.	

H C Welch Major
ADVS. 30th Div

Instructions regarding War Diaries and Intelligence Summaries are contained in F. S. Regs., Part II. and the Staff Manual respectively. Title pages will be prepared in manuscript.

WAR DIARY
or
INTELLIGENCE SUMMARY.
(Erase heading not required.)

Army Form C. 2118.

ADVS 30 Div
February
Vol 4

Place	Date	Hour	Summary of Events and Information	Remarks and references to Appendices
Etinehem	Feb 1		Inspected 15th Infantry Brigade, Bray also 27th Bde R.F.A. Bois de Tailles.	
	2		Sergt Nutley A V C (No 1711 reported at this Office for duty with D Battery 149 Bde R.F.A.	
			Inspected B Battery 151 Bde R.F.A. and C Battery 149 Bois de Tailles - Visited No. 40 Mobile V Sectn	
	3		Inspected 1/1 Lancs Bde R.G.A. Bois de Tailles.	
	4		Inspected Ammunition Column 150th Brigade R.F.A.	
	5		Visited Bois de Tailles - inspected A Battery 149th Bde R.F.A.	
			A.V.S visited Etinehem - also D.D.V.S. 3rd Army re case of Glanders in "A" Battery 149.	
			Placed A Battery in isolation for testing with Mallein.	
			No 40 Mobile Veterinary Section put out of bounds owing to the case of Glanders in "A" Battery 149 Bde being in the Section. All animals in Section tested with Mallein.	
	6		Visited Bois de Tailles - Malleining horses of A Battery 149 Bde R.F.A.	
	7		Inspecting horses of A Battery 149 Bde R.F.A. Two doubtful reactors in Battery isolated	
	8		" " " " " " " " All passed the test excepting the two isolated	
	9		" " " " " " " " Retested doubtful reactors.	
			Inspected horses 29th Bde R.G.A. on Chipilly Rd also 148 Ammunition Column. Bois de Tailles.	

2353 Wt. W2544/1454 700,000 5/15 D. D. & L. A.D.S.S. Forms/C. 2118.

Volume 4
Feb 29 1916
H Clu[illegible] Maj[illegible]
[illegible] 30th [illegible]

Instructions regarding War Diaries and Intelligence Summaries are contained in F. S. Regs., Part II. and the Staff Manual respectively. Title pages will be prepared in manuscript.

WAR DIARY
or
INTELLIGENCE SUMMARY.
(Erase heading not required.)

Army Form C. 2118.

Place	Date	Hour	Summary of Events and Information	Remarks and references to Appendices
Etinehem	Feb 10		Saw G.O.C. 30th Divisional H.d Q.trs reference the animals of this Division	
			Visited Bois de Tailles. Inspected 21st Infantry Brigade Transport at Bray.	
	11		Called on C R A about the watering arrangements of horses in Etinehem being very unsatisfactory – drew attention to this at H. Qtrs Division –	
			Inspected A Battery 148 Bde R.F.A. also B Battery 151st Bde on the Etinehem, Bray Road.	
	12		Visited Bois de Tailles inspecting 149 Bde R F A	
			No 40 Mobile V Section moved to Sailly Laurette Road from Etinehem	
	13		Captain Fyrth A V C of 5th Division reported himself	
			Visited Mobile V. Section Chipilly	
	14		Inspected H Qtrs animals in Etinehem – Inspected Batteries of 148 149 & 150 Bdes R.F.A in Bois de Tailles	
	15		Visited Chipilly inspecting animals of Lancashire Hussars –	
	16		In Office	
	17		Inspected 200 & 202 Coys R.E. at Bray also 11 South Lancs.	
	18		Inspected Divisional Ammunition Column at Chipilly	

Instructions regarding War Diaries and Intelligence Summaries are contained in F. S. Regs., Part II. and the Staff Manual respectively. Title pages will be prepared in manuscript.

WAR DIARY
or
INTELLIGENCE SUMMARY.
(Erase heading not required.)

Army Form C. 2118.

Place	Date	Hour	Summary of Events and Information	Remarks and references to Appendices
Etinehem	Feb. 19		Inspected No 40 Mobile V Section on Sailly Laurette Rd	
"	20		Visited " " " " " " " " "	
			Inspected C Battery 149 Bde Bois de Tailles Inspected 65th Howitzer Battery on the Cappy Suzanne Road also D Battery 151 Bde R.F.A.	
	21		Inspected B Battery 148 Bde R.F.A	
			" H'Qrs Divisional Signal Coy animals.	
	22		Inspected 1/6 1/7 Black Watch transport animals at Bray. - also A Battery 149 Bde R.F.A Bois de Tailles	
	23		Visited M.V.S at Sailly Laurette Road	
			With Captain Williamson A.V.C in Office handing over correspondence etc prior to my departure on leave on the 24th	
	24		Handed over Office to Captain Williamson A.V.C who is acting as A.D.V.S. of this Division whilst I go on leave	
	25		Departed on 10 days leave	

H.C. Welch
Major
A.D.V.S 30th Divn

2353 Wt. W2544/1454 700,000 5/15 D. D. & L. A.D.S.S. Forms/C 2118.

Army Form C. 2118.

Instructions regarding War Diaries and Intelligence Summaries are contained in F. S. Regs., Part II. and the Staff Manual respectively. Title pages will be prepared in manuscript.

WAR DIARY
or
INTELLIGENCE SUMMARY.
(Erase heading not required.)

Place	Date	Hour	Summary of Events and Information	Remarks and references to Appendices
Stienheim	12/3/16		Returned from leave	
" "	13		D.D.V.S. 4th Army called. Visited B. Battery 148 Bde R.F.A. in the Bois de Tailles.	
" "			Called on Staff Captain Hd Qrs Artillery re mallening B. Battery horses 148 Bde R.F.A.	
" "	14		Visited Bois de Tailles inspected C & D. Batteries 150 Bde. also B & C. Batteries 149 Bde. — Supervised the testing with mallein B. Battery 148 Bde R.F.A. Called at Hd Qrs Divisional — informed C.R.A. of the poor condition of the horses of 149 Bde generally.	
" "	15		Visited B. Battery 151 Bde R.F.A. Bois de Tailles also C. Battery 150 Bde	
" "	16		Visited A. Battery 150 Bde at Bray. Called on G.O.C. the Division re the bad watering arrangements for horses generally in Stienheim. Bois de Tailles &c	
" "	17		Inspected Brigade Ammunition Column 149 Bde R.F.A. on the Cabbly Suzanne Rd. Inspected 183 Tunnelling Co at Bray.	
" "	18		Inspected Bde Ammunition Column 148 Bde R.F.A. in Bois de Tailles. Inspected 1/1 Lanes R.G.A. Chipilly Rd. also 1/2 Lanes R.G.A.	
"	19		Visited Mobile Veterinary Section (40) on the Sailly-le-Sec Rd.	
"	20		Hd Qrs 30th Division left Stienheim for Montigny — Received instructions to make	

Volume 5
March 31.3.16
H. Endell Major
OC VS 30th Bn

Instructions regarding War Diaries and Intelligence Summaries are contained in F. S. Regs., Part II. and the Staff Manual respectively. Title pages will be prepared in manuscript.

WAR DIARY
or
INTELLIGENCE SUMMARY.
(Erase heading not required.)

Army Form C. 2118.

Place	Date	Hour	Summary of Events and Information	Remarks and references to Appendices
Sturchem	20 3/16		to make my Head Quarters at Daours pointed to A.Q.M.G. this was not the most efficient arrangement for carrying out my duties	
DAOURS.	21 3/16		Left Sturchem at 3 P.m. for Daours. Car arranged to call at 10 am. Arrived Daours 4 15 P.m.	
" "	22		Arranging accommodation for No 40. Mobile V. Section. No 40. Mobile V Section arrived Daours at 3.30 P.m	
" "	23		Inspected C Battery and Ammunition Column 150 Bde R.F.A. Daours. Went to a Conference at D.D.V.S.' Office Head Quarters 3rd Army.	
" "	24		Colonel Hunt D.D.V.S. 4th Army called.	
" "	25		Inspected 30 Divisional Ammunition Column at Bussy le Daours	
" "	26		D.D.V.S. 4th Army called & visited No 40. Mobile V Section.	
" "	27		Captain Williamson A.V.C. i/c 40 Mobile V Section went on leave. Colonel Hunt D.D.V.S visited 40 Mobile V Section - had destroyed three horses of 150 Brigade Ammunition suspected of Glanders. P.M. revealed same.	
AILLY sur-Somme	28		Left Daours for AILLY-sur-Somme where H.Qrs of the Division are proceeding. Arrived Ailly-sur-Somme 4 P.m.	

2353 Wt. W2544/1454 700,000 5/15 D. D. & L. A.D.S.S. Forms/C. 2118.

Instructions regarding War Diaries and Intelligence Summaries are contained in F. S. Regs., Part II. and the Staff Manual respectively. Title pages will be prepared in manuscript.

Army Form C. 2118.

WAR DIARY
or
INTELLIGENCE SUMMARY.
(Erase heading not required.)

Place	Date	Hour	Summary of Events and Information	Remarks and references to Appendices
Ailly sur Somme	29 3/16		Visited Picquigny inspected 96 Field Ambulance. Inspected 97. Field Ambulance at Allonville.	
"	30 3/16		Visited 40 Mobile V. Section at St. Sauveur and 98 Field Ambulance at Bertangles.	
"	31 3/16		" " " " " " " " " also 90th Bde H.Q. Corbie – 16th Manchesters Corbie – 17th Manchesters Bonnay. 18th Manchesters at Frechencourt. 200 Field Company R.E. also	

H. Clutch [?]
Major
ADVS 30th Division
31. 3. 16

2353 Wt. W2544/1454 700,000 5/15 D. D. & L. A.D.S.S. Forms/C. 2118.

1916

Instructions regarding War Diaries and Intelligence Summaries are contained in F. S. Regs., Part II. and the Staff Manual respectively. Title pages will be prepared in manuscript.

WAR DIARY
or
INTELLIGENCE SUMMARY.
(Erase heading not required.)

Army Form C. 2118.

Place	Date	Hour	Summary of Events and Information	Remarks and references to Appendices
AILLY sur Somme				
DAOURS	1st June		Inspected 2nd Welsh Transport animals at Picquigny - also 21st Infantry Bde Machine Gun Corps.	
			Inspected 19th Manchester Breilly	
" "	2		Visited No 40. Mobile V. Section St. Sauveur - Inspected Transport animals 2nd Yorks	
			Inspected transport animals 18th Liverpools at Vaux also 203 Company Divisional Train at	
" "	3		Inspected 201 Co R.E. at Picquigny - also Lancashire Hussars at Breilly	
			Visited No 40. Mobile V. Section at St. Sauveur	
" "	4		Inspected Bde Ammunition Column 150 Bde R.F.A. Visited No 40. Mobile V Section	
" "	5		Inspected B and C Batteries and Brigade Ammunition Column 148 Bde R.F.A. also	
			D and C Batteries 150 Bde R.F.A. Argoeuvres	
" "	6		Visited No 40. Mobile V. Section - Lancashire Hussars - also Hd Qrs Divisional Signal Coy at Picquigny	
" "	7		In Office	
" "	8		Inspected 30th Divisional Train at Longpre	
" "	9		Lieut Keston V.O. 150 Bde R.F.A met with an accident - admitted to Hospital	
			Inspected 96. Field Ambulance at Picquigny	
" "	10		Inspected C Battery 148 Bde R.F.A at Argoeuvres	

Volume 6

June 30: 1916

Handed in

a.k.v.s. 30 [illegible]

Army Form C. 2118.

Instructions regarding War Diaries and Intelligence Summaries are contained in F. S. Regs., Part II. and the Staff Manual respectively. Title pages will be prepared in manuscript.

WAR DIARY
or
INTELLIGENCE SUMMARY.
(Erase heading not required.)

Place	Date	Hour	Summary of Events and Information	Remarks and references to Appendices
AILLY. SUR Somme en DAO [illegible]	11th April		Inspected 98th Field Ambulance at Bertangles	
"	12		Lieut Lowe AVC reported himself for duty with 150 Bde R.F.A.	
"	13		Visited 4th Gn Divisional Signals	
"	14		Inspected 16 Manchester at Bussy. Lieut Lowe AVC reported his departure for 1st Army.	
"	15		Called on C R A at Argoeuves	
"	16		Visited 16th Manchester	
"	17		Visited 2nd Royal Scot Fusiliers at Flesselles also 90th Bde Machine G Co at Vaux	
			DDVS 4th Army called	
"	18		Visited No 40 M.V.S.	
"	19		Visited 98 Field Ambulance at Bertangles also 202 Co R.E.	
			Inspected D Battery 148 at St Sauveur	
"	20th		Visited 21st Machine G Co Picquigny – B A and D. Batteries 150 Bde R.F.A Argoeuves	
			B and D batteries 149 Bde R.F.A	
"	21		Inspected 19 Manchester Bn at St Sauveur – also No 40. M.V.S.	
"	22		Visited 90th Infantry Bde at Picquigny	
"	23		Inspected 11th South Lancs at Vaux	

Instructions regarding War Diaries and Intelligence Summaries are contained in F. S. Regs., Part II. and the Staff Manual respectively. Title pages will be prepared in manuscript.

WAR DIARY
or
INTELLIGENCE SUMMARY.
(Erase heading not required.)

Army Form C. 2118.

A D V S
30 Div
Vol 6

Place	Date	Hour	Summary of Events and Information	Remarks and references to Appendices
AILLY SUR SOMME	24/4/16		Visited Mobile Veterinary Section at St Sauveur. also 90th Infantry Bde at Picquigny.	
" "	25th		Inspected Divisional Ammunition Column at Argoeuves. also A and D Batteries 149 Bde R.F.A	
" "	26		Inspected 21st Bde Machine Gun Company at Picquigny. 202 Co R.E. also transport animals 18th Manchesters	
" "	27		Visited Mobile V. Section with D.D.V.S. 4th Army.	
" "	28		Inspected D. Battery 149 Bde D. 150 Bde. B. 149. and Brigade Ammunition Column 149 Bde	
" "	29		Inspected the Shoeing of Divisional Ammunition Column Argoeuves	
" "	30		Inspected Lancashire Hussars at Breilly.	

H. Cowell.
Major.
ADVS 30th Division

2353 Wt. W2544/1454 700,000 5/15 D. D. & L. A.D.S.S. Forms/C 2118.

Instructions regarding War Diaries and Intelligence Summaries are contained in F. S. Regs., Part II. and the Staff Manual respectively. Title pages will be prepared in manuscript.

WAR DIARY
or
INTELLIGENCE SUMMARY.
(Erase heading not required.)

Army Form C. 2118.

Place	Date	Hour	Summary of Events and Information	Remarks and references to Appendices
Ailly Sur Somme	May 1		Lieut Stokes AVC reported for duty with 150 Bde R F A.	
			Visited No 40 Mobile V. Section at St. Sauveur.	
" "	" 2		Inspected animals 30th Divisional Ammunition at Argoeuves	
" "	" 3		Inspected B and D Batteries 149 Bde R F A at Argoeuves. D.D.V.S called and	
			visited No 40 Mobile V. Section St. Sauveur	
" "	" 4		In Office	
" "	" 5		Left Ailly-Sur-Somme at 10. am for Etinehem with Head Qrs 30th Division	
			arrived Etinehem 12.20. pm.	
Etinehem	" 6		Inspected C Battery 149 Bde and Section D.A.C at La Neuville.	
			Inspected A Battery 151 Bde on Bray Etinehem Rd	
" "	" 7		Inspected Brigade Ammunition Column 148 Bde R F A in the Bois de Tailles	
			" " B Battery 151 Bde Bois de Tailles and Brigade Ammunition Column	
			" " 12th Battery R.G.A Chipilly Rd	
" "	8		Inspected B Battery 149 Bde A and B 148 Bde also B 150 Bde in the Bois de Tailles.	
" "	9		attended a conference at D.D.V.S office H Qrs 4th Army.	
" "	10		Inspected Lancashire Hussars at Chipilly.	

Volume 4.
May 31. 16
H. Uuclch [illegible]
Major

Army Form C. 2118.

Instructions regarding War Diaries and Intelligence Summaries are contained in F. S. Regs., Part II. and the Staff Manual respectively. Title pages will be prepared in manuscript.

WAR DIARY
or
INTELLIGENCE SUMMARY.
(Erase heading not required.)

Place	Date	Hour	Summary of Events and Information	Remarks and references to Appendices
Etinehem	May 11th		Inspected Hd Qrs Divisional Signals	
			Inspected A B and D Batteries 82nd Bde R.F.A. of 18th Division at the Bois des Tailles also C Battery 148 on Bray Etinehem Rd. also D and A Batteries 85th Bde R.F.A 18th Division	
"	May 12		Inspecting A B C & D Batteries 150 Bde R.F.A	
"	" 13		Inspecting 89th Infantry Bde at Bray & La Neuville – also 200 Field Co R.E.	
"	" 14		Inspecting 124 Bde R.G.A. at La Neuville – 79 Co R.E. (18th Division) at Sailly Laurette.	
"	15		Visiting B Battery 149. Bde Bois de Tailles and B Battery 148 Bde.	
			Inspected Divisional Ammun Column 18th Division.	
			Lieut A H Clark AVC died result of a Railway accident	
"	16		Inspected 82 Bde R.F.A 18th Division –	
			At the Bois de Tailles exchanging horses of Units with surplus horses of 30th Divisional Artillery.	
"	17		Inspecting horses of 150 B A C and 149 Bde R.F.A proceeding to Albert –	
			Sent 34 Animals into 40 Mobile V Section –	

2353 Wt. W2544/1454 700,000 5/15 D. D. & L. A.D.S.S. Forms/C. 2118.

Instructions regarding War Diaries and Intelligence Summaries are contained in F. S. Regs., Part II. and the Staff Manual respectively. Title pages will be prepared in manuscript.

WAR DIARY
or
INTELLIGENCE SUMMARY.
(Erase heading not required.)

Army Form C. 2118.

Place	Date	Hour	Summary of Events and Information	Remarks and references to Appendices
Etinehem	18/5/16		Inspected B C and D Batteries 149 Bde R F A. with Captain Clunes AVC	
			Visited 1/40 Mobile V. Section Sailly Laurette	
	19th		Inspected D A C 30th Division in Bois de Tailles & Chipilly	
			Called on the G. O. C.	
	20th		Visited 82nd Bde R F A with Captain Williams AVC also 12th Battery R. G. A. with Sergt Shannon.	
"	21st		Inspected 55th Transport animals 7th Buffs. Stainton Camp.	
			Inspected Transport animals of Duke of Cornwalls Light Infantry at Chipilly.	
	22		Inspected horses 30th Divisional Train at [illegible].	
			" B Battery 148 Bde in the Bois de Tailles	
	23		Inspected No 1 Section Divisional Ammunition Column 18th Division in Bois de Tailles	
	"		Inspected 150 Bde R F A also A & C Batteries Bois de Tailles	
			Inspected 96 and 97 Field Ambulances at Sailly Laurette.	
	24		Inspected 7th Entrenching Bn Bois de Tailles	
			Inspected 20th Division at Bray. XX. Cable Section Stainton and A M Cable Section Bois de Tailles. Had watering troughs & pump fixed in extension at side of River owing to the watering arrangements being insufficient for the units in this area.	

Instructions regarding War Diaries and Intelligence Summaries are contained in F. S. Regs., Part II. and the Staff Manual respectively. Title pages will be prepared in manuscript.

WAR DIARY
or
INTELLIGENCE SUMMARY.
(Erase heading not required.)

Army Form C. 2118.

Place	Date	Hour	Summary of Events and Information	Remarks and references to Appendices
Etinehem	25th		Inspected 12 Middlesex Regiment - Sussex Pioneers and 7th Bedfords of the 18th Division in Bray - also 6th Berks 8th Suffolks & 53 Machine Gun Company.	
			Inspected 2nd Royal Scot Fusiliers - 202 Co R.E. 11th South Lancs and 16 & 17th Manchester Bns in and around Bray.	
			Inspected following units 18th Division 79 & 80 Coy R.E. and No 4 Section DAC Bray.	
〃	26th		Visited H.Q. Mobile V. Section Sailly Laurette.	
			Visited Bois des Tailles with Captain Williamson AVC selecting a site for advanced collecting station for Section.	
			Pte Salthouse F. No 158507. A.P.C. clerk to relieve present clerk in ADVS' office.	
〃	27		Visited Bois des Tailles inspected B Battery 83 Bde RFA and B. 85th Bde of the 18th Division - also A Battery 149 Bde R.F.A.	
			Inspected 89th Bde Machine Gun Co Etinehem.	
	28		Visited 30th Divisional Train School.	
〃	29		Inspected B battery 151 Bde R.F.A. B battery 149 Bde also D149 and D battery 82 Bde R.F.A. 18th Division	

2353 Wt. W2544/1454 700,000 5/15 D. D. & L. A.D.S.S. Forms/C. 2118.

Instructions regarding War Diaries and Intelligence Summaries are contained in F. S. Regs., Part II. and the Staff Manual respectively. Title pages will be prepared in manuscript.

WAR DIARY
or
INTELLIGENCE SUMMARY.

(Erase heading not required.)

Army Form C. 2118.

A.D.V.S. 30th Div
Vol 7

Place	Date	Hour	Summary of Events and Information	Remarks and references to Appendices
Etinehem	May 30		Pte Willet AVC Clerk in ADVS' Office sent to 40. Mobile V. Section in accordance with instructions received from O/c AVC Records Base.	
"	31.		Proceeding on leave. Captain Williamson AVC took over ADVS' Office.	

H Clarke
Major
ADVS 30th Division

2353 Wt. W2544/1454 700,000 5/15 D. D. & L. A.D.S.S. Forms/C. 2118.

Instructions regarding War Diaries and Intelligence Summaries are contained in F. S. Regs., Part II. and the Staff Manual respectively. Title pages will be prepared in manuscript.

Army Form C. 2118.

WAR DIARY
or
INTELLIGENCE SUMMARY.
(Erase heading not required.)

Place	Date 1916	Hour	Summary of Events and Information	Remarks and references to Appendices
ETINEHEM	1-6		Visited 40th mobile Vety Section	
	2-6		Office work	
	3-6		Inspected transport of 6th Bn R. Berks. 8th Bn Suffolks, 8th Bn Norfolks, 10th Bn Essex.	
	4-6		Office work visited 40th M.V.S.	
	5-6		Inspected wagon lines of 1/1 Lancs R.G.A., 12 Heavy Battery R.G.A. Visited 40th M.V.S.	
	6-6		Inspected horses no 1 Coy 30th Divisional Train, visited 40th M.V.S.	
	7-6		Office work, inspected 124 Heavy Battery R.G.A	
	7-6		Inspected 90th Inf Bde machine Gun Coy	
	9-6		Office work	
	10-6		Visited 40th M.V.S. Inspected C. Batty 151 Bde R.F.A. & C. Batty 150th Bde R.F.A.	
	" "		Major H C. Welch ADVS 30th Division returned from leave.	
	11-6		In Office	
	12-6		Inspected 84th Bde R.F.A. of 18th Divisional Artillery Bois-de-Tailles	
			Inspected 149 Bde R.F.A. Bois-de-Tailles.	
	13-6		Inspected 150 Bde R.F.A " " " " also C. Battery 151 -	
			Visited Mobile V Section Sailly Laurette inspecting horses for evacuation.	

Volume 8.

H.C. Welch Maj.

AKVS 30th Kn

June 30. 1916

Instructions regarding War Diaries and Intelligence Summaries are contained in F. S. Regs., Part II. and the Staff Manual respectively. Title pages will be prepared in manuscript.

WAR DIARY
or
INTELLIGENCE SUMMARY.
(Erase heading not required.)

Army Form C. 2118.

Place	Date	Hour	Summary of Events and Information	Remarks and references to Appendices
	1916			
Etinehem	14.6.		Inspected C. Battery 151. Bde A148 - C 148 Bois-de-Tailles	
			Inspected 115 R.G.A and 31st Battery R.G.A Chipilly Rd.	
" "	15.6		Inspected the following Batteries in the Bois-de-Tailles B.151 - D.150 - D149.	
" "	16.6		Visited 40 Mobile V. Section Sailly Laurette. Hd Qrs Divisional Signals	
			Called on the C.R.A 30th Division pointing the poor condition of many of the horses of the Divisional Artillery due to the excessive work they are having - Went with C.R.A and saw the following batteries C.151 - C.149 C150. &c.	
" "	17.6		D.D.V.S. 4th Army called: Visited 6th Siege Battery R.G.A. on the Bray Corbie Rd. No 40. Mobile V. Section moved to Corbie	
" "	18.6		Inspected 89th Infantry Bde also 17th Manchesters and 11th South Lancs on the Bray Etinehem Rd. Went to conference at D.D.V.S' office Head Quarters 4th Army.	
" "	19.6		Visited Advanced Mobile V Section in the Bois-de-Tailles	
			Visited 83 Bde R.F.A 18th Division. Called on Staff Captain R.A	

Instructions regarding War Diaries and Intelligence Summaries are contained in F. S. Regs., Part II. and the Staff Manual respectively. Title pages will be prepared in manuscript.

WAR DIARY
or
INTELLIGENCE SUMMARY.
(Erase heading not required.)

Army Form C. 2118.

Place	Date	Hour	Summary of Events and Information	Remarks and references to Appendices
	1916			
Vlinchun	19.6		Inspected 200. 201 and 202 Field Companies R.E. at Bray. Called on the General Officer Commanding 30th Division pointing out the bad condition of many of the horses of the 30th Divisional Artillery - also the very hard work they are called upon to do.	
" "	20.6		Inspected 2nd and 3rd Battalions South African Infantry Sluchen Camp. Visited Mobile Vet Section No 40 Corbie - also No 40 Advanced Veterinary Section Bois des Tailles - Inspected 1/1 Lanes R.G.A. Chipilly Rd	
" "	21.6		Inspected 149 Bde R.F.A. Bois-des-Tailles also A. B. and C. Batteries 150 Bde R.F.A. Inspected B. Battery 84 Bde R.F.A. (18 Division) and C Battery 151. Bde R.F.A. (30th Div) Bois de Tailles	
" "	22 6		Inspected B. Echelon 30th Divisional Ammunition Column Sailly Laurette - also 96. 97 and 98 Field Ambulances. Visited No 40 Advanced Veterinary Section Bois de Tailles inspecting horses for evacuation.	
" "	23.6		Inspected animals 149 Bde R.F.A. Bois de Tailles 201st Field Co R.E. Bray - Several mules on the horse gris.	

2353 Wt. W2544/1454 700,000 5/15 D. D. & L. A.D.S.S. Forms/C. 2118.

Instructions regarding War Diaries and Intelligence Summaries are contained in F. S. Regs., Part II. and the Staff Manual respectively. Title pages will be prepared in manuscript.

WAR DIARY
or
INTELLIGENCE SUMMARY.
(Erase heading not required.)

Army Form C. 2118.

Place	Date	Hour	Summary of Events and Information	Remarks and references to Appendices
	1916			
Sturchem	23.6		Inspected Transport animals 21st Infantry Bde at Bray.	
" "	24.6		Visited advanced Veterinary Section Bois-de-Tailles	
" "	" "		Visited C and B. batteries 149 Bde R.F.A. Bois de Tailles	
" "	25.6		Visited B. battery 149 Bde. Inspected 31st 124 and 115 Batteries R.F.A. ~~Bois de~~ Chibilly Rd.	
" "	26.6		Visited advanced V Section. 149 Bde R.F.A. B. battery 151. Bde and C and A batteries 150 Bdes.	
" "	27.6		Inspected animals at Advanced Veterinary Section for evacuation	
			Inspected C. Battery 151 Bois de Tailles. This battery has horses on the light side.	
			" " D " " 149 " " " some horses on the light side	
			" " D " " 151 " " "	
			Inspected animals of 16th Manchesters. also 17th Manchesters Sturchem.	
" "	28.6		Inspected 2 Royal Scot Fusiliers. 18th Manchesters. 90 Bde Machine Gun Section in valley on Bray Sturchem Rd.	
" "	29.6		Inspected A and C Batteries 148 Bde R.F.A. C and B batteries 149 in Bois de Tailles.	
" "	30.6		Inspected A battery 149 Bde R.F.A. also C.150. many horses in poor condition belonging to these batteries.	

2353 Wt. W2544/1454 700,000 5/15 D. D. & L. A.D.S.S. Forms/C. 2118.

ADVS. 30 Div

Army Form C. 2118.

Vol 8

Instructions regarding War Diaries and Intelligence Summaries are contained in F. S. Regs., Part II. and the Staff Manual respectively. Title pages will be prepared in manuscript.

WAR DIARY
or
INTELLIGENCE SUMMARY.
(Erase heading not required.)

Place	Date	Hour	Summary of Events and Information	Remarks and references to Appendices
	1916			
Stuchem	30/6		Note to A A Q M G. 30th Division drawing attention to the poor condition of many of the horses of the Divisional artillery. Copy sent to C.R.A. also pointing out that I am continually evacuating animals from artillery units. Inspected animals for evacuation from 40 advanced V. Section Bois de Tailles.	
			H C Welch Maj. ADVS 30th Div	

Instructions regarding War Diaries and Intelligence Summaries are contained in F. S. Regs., Part II. and the Staff Manual respectively. Title pages will be prepared in manuscript.

Army Form C. 2118.

WAR DIARY
or
INTELLIGENCE SUMMARY.
(Erase heading not required.)

Place	Date	Hour	Summary of Events and Information	Remarks and references to Appendices
	1916			
Sterchem	July 1st		Visited No 40 advanced Veterinary Section and inspected horses for evacuation — In office remainder of day	
"	2		Visited Bois de Tailles inspecting the following units C Battery 150 Bde R.F.A. A Battery 149 — many of the horses of this battery are in poor condition although they have been hard worked this is not the cause entirely but in my opinion want of supervision which I am constantly pointing out.	
"	3		Inspected transport animals of Head Quarters Signals Sterchem. Inspected following units Bois de Tailles — A. B. C. batteries 149 Bde R.F.A. Camp D. 151 — B and C 150 Bde R.F.A. Inspected animals for evacuation from 40 advanced Veterinary Section.	
"	4		Visited Grove Town Camp and inspected the following units 200 201 202. 238 and 232 Field Coy R.E. also Grenade transport animals. Visited Bois de Tailles and inspected transport animals of the 89th 90th and 21st Infantry Bdes.	
"	5		Visited No 40 advanced Veterinary Section and inspected horses for evacuation. Visited 149 Bde R.F.A. Bois de Tailles — also C battery 150. Inspected 40. Mobile Veterinary Section at Corbie —	

2353 Wt. W2544/1454 700,000 5/15 D. D. & L. A.D.S.S. Forms/C. 2118.

4° 938 / 5.8.16

Volume 9.
Ending July 31st 1916.
H Cheldi.
Major.
ADVS.
30th Division

Army Form C. 2118.

Instructions regarding War Diaries and Intelligence Summaries are contained in F. S. Regs., Part II. and the Staff Manual respectively. Title pages will be prepared in manuscript.

WAR DIARY
or
INTELLIGENCE SUMMARY.
(Erase heading not required.)

Place	Date	Hour	Summary of Events and Information	Remarks and references to Appendices
	1916			
Etinehem	July 6		Visited No 40 Advanced Veterinary Section and inspected horses for Evacuation.	
			Visited Sailly Laurette and inspected horses of 30th Divisional Train	
"	" 7		D.D.V.S. 4th Army called. Went with D.D.V.S. to the Bois de Tailles and inspected some of the horses of the 30th Divisional Artillery	
"	" 8		Visited Bois de Tailles and inspected A B and C Batteries 149 Bde R.F.A. A dozen horses of C Battery in poor condition - 8 in B - and several in A.	
"	" "		Visited Advanced Veterinary Section and inspected horses for Evacuation.	
"	" 9		Visited Bois-de-Tailles and inspected 11th South Lancs also 89th and 21st Infantry Bdes. In the 19th Manchesters several horses in poor condition.	
"	" 10		Visited No 40 Advanced V. Section Bois de Tailles. Inspected D. Battery 148 Bde R.F.A also No 1 Section DAC Bois-de-Tailles	
"	" 11		Visited Copse Valley and inspected 149 Bde R.F.A. In B and C Batteries are a number of poor horses and both batteries are in poor condition and have fallen off very much this last few days also inspected C and A Batteries 150 Bde R.F.A ~~at~~ and B Battery 151 Bde.	
"	" "		Visited Advanced Veterinary Section Bois de Tailles.	

Instructions regarding War Diaries and Intelligence Summaries are contained in F. S. Regs., Part II. and the Staff Manual respectively. Title pages will be prepared in manuscript.

WAR DIARY
or
INTELLIGENCE SUMMARY.
(Erase heading not required.)

Army Form C. 2118.

Place	Date	Hour	Summary of Events and Information	Remarks and references to Appendices
	1916			
Sluncheon	July 12		Inspected transport animals of the 90th Infantry Bde in the Bois-de-Celestine sent several animals to Hospital.	
			Inspected the M. P. Bois de Celestine - evacuated one case for mange	
" "	13		Inspected A B + C batteries 149 Bde R.F.A. in Copse Valley - the condition generally of this Bde is not good -	
			Visited 40 Mobile V. Section Bois-de-Tailles	
" "	14		Left Sluncheon at 1 P.m. Divisional Head Quarters removing to Corbie - Arrived Corbie 2.30 P.m.	
Corbie	15		Inspected H.Q. Qrs animals of the 89th Infantry Bde at Corbie sent two mules to Hospital -	
			Inspected 17th Kings Liverpool Regiment evacuated one animal for mange.	
" "	16		Inspected transport animals of 200 and 202 Field Co R.E. at Vaux also 201 Field Co R.E at DAOURS.	
			Visited Vaux and inspected transport animals of the 19th and 20th Bns Liverpool Regts also 2nd Bedfordshire Regiment	

2353 Wt. W2544/1454 700,000 5/15 D. D. & L. A.D.S.S./Forms/C. 2118.

Instructions regarding War Diaries and Intelligence Summaries are contained in F. S. Regs., Part II. and the Staff Manual respectively. Title pages will be prepared in manuscript.

WAR DIARY
or
INTELLIGENCE SUMMARY.
(Erase heading not required.)

Army Form C. 2118.

Place	Date	Hour	Summary of Events and Information	Remarks and references to Appendices
	1916			
Corbie	July 17		Inspected 89 Bde Machine Gun Comp at Corbie	
			Visited Daours and inspected transport animals 18th Bn Manchester Regt also 201 Field Co R E	
" "	18		Visited Daours for the purpose of inspecting and reporting on nose bags with the zinc recently issued to some units - They are too narrow and deep the edges are not rounded off as in the old pattern - wounds and swellings are caused thereby on the side of the neck - Sent a report about same to Q. branch - also sent a copy to D.D.V.S. 4th Army.	
			Visited Head Qrs 89 Infantry Bde for the purpose of seeing two chargers - Sent one to 40 Mobile V. Section - also another of Head Qrs 90 Infantry Bde.	
" "	19		Visited Bois de Tailles and inspected animals in 40 Mobile V. Section for evacuation - D.D.V.S. 4th Army called.	
" "	20		Left Corbie with H Qrs 30th Division	
			Arrived at Billon Copse L.16.c.5.5 at 6.30 P.m.	
	21		In office.	
	22		Inspected 148 Bde R.F.A. in Bois des Tailles with A and B batteries - Sent 7 horses from these batteries to the Mobile V Section for debility.	

Instructions regarding War Diaries and Intelligence Summaries are contained in F. S. Regs., Part II. and the Staff Manual respectively. Title pages will be prepared in manuscript.

Army Form C. 2118.

WAR DIARY
or
INTELLIGENCE SUMMARY.
(Erase heading not required.)

Place	Date	Hour	Summary of Events and Information	Remarks and references to Appendices
Battle dug out L.16.b.53	1916 July 23		Inspected A B and C batteries 150 Bde R.F.A in Bois-de-Tailles N. condition generally fairly good – Sent 3 horses to Mobile V. Section for wounds etc – Visited Mobile V. Section Bois de Tailles N. and inspected some 54 animals for evacuation. Sergt R. Hobbs A.V.C. reported for duty	
" "	" 24		Visited Bois de Tailles N inspected B. Echelon. 30th D.A.C – condition generally good. also inspected A and B. batteries 148 Bde R.F.A – evacuated 2 horses from A Battery to Section for debility Sergt R. Hobbs A.V.C. posted to 149 Bde R.F.A.	
" "	" 25		Visited F.22.c and inspected the horses of 149. Bde R.F.A A battery condition fair – D good. B poor – evacuated from this battery 3 horses in very poor condition – C. battery has improved since I last saw it. Inspected 151st Bde R.F.A. A battery in very good condition B. light – also some of C battery. Visited 40 Mobile V. Section Bois de Tailles at L.2.c.8.6 – and inspected 16 horses for evacuation to base	

Instructions regarding War Diaries and Intelligence Summaries are contained in F. S. Regs., Part II. and the Staff Manual respectively. Title pages will be prepared in manuscript.

WAR DIARY
or
INTELLIGENCE SUMMARY.
(Erase heading not required.)

Army Form C. 2118.

Place	Date	Hour	Summary of Events and Information	Remarks and references to Appendices
	1916			
Battle Bingoots	July 25		Visited No 40 Mobile V. Section Bois de Tailles H. and inspected 53 animals for Evacuation.	
			Visited Happy Valley selecting site for No 40 Advanced Collecting Station	
	26		Advanced collecting Station situated at L 2 c 8 6	
			Inspected transport animals of 21st Infantry Bde in Happy Valley. also 89th Infantry Bde –	
	27		Left Battle Bingoots 10 30 am. Arrived Bray Albert Rd at F 26 d 1.1 at 11 am –	
Bray Albert Rd			Inspected the following Batteries R. F. A. Nos 124 – 115 31st 12th and 6th.	
F 26 d 1.1			Received telegram from D.D.V.S. 4th Army to attend Conference at 2.30 P.m on the 28th inst	
" "	28		Inspected 90th Infantry Bde in Happy Valley.	
			Unable to attend D.D.V.S. Conference – no car available	
			Interviewed all V.Os re returns –	
" "	29		Visited 148 Bde R F A and inspected B and C Batteries	
			Visited 149 Bde R F A and inspected C battery	
			Visited 40 Mobile V Section inspecting horses for Evacuation	
			Visited No 40 Advanced Veterinary Section.	
" "	30		Inspected A and B batteries 150 Bde R F A also Visited 40 Mobile Veterinary Section Bois de Tailles H.	

2353 Wt. W2544/1454 700,000 5/15 D. D. & L. A.D.S.S. Forms/C. 2118.

34 July

Instructions regarding War Diaries and Intelligence Summaries are contained in F. S. Regs., Part II. and the Staff Manual respectively. Title pages will be prepared in manuscript.

WAR DIARY
or
INTELLIGENCE SUMMARY.
(Erase heading not required.)

Army Form C. 2118.

A.D.V.S.
Vol 9

Place	Date	Hour	Summary of Events and Information	Remarks and references to Appendices
Bray + Albert Rd	1916 31 July		Inspected 149 Bde R.F.A at F.22.d.3.1. There are a number of poor horses in this Bde confined mostly to A and B. batteries. Instructing the Veterinary Officer i/c to send the following animals to the Mobile V. Section for debility A 55. 32. 91 — B. 40. 43. 53. 139. 71. 18. 89 also C. 82. + 92. There are a number of horses still remaining that should be evacuated but owing to the Bde being under strength I am unable to do so.	
			Visited 40. Mobile V. Section and inspected 16 animals for evacuation.	
			H. Cl[illegible] Major ADVS. 30th Division	

2353 Wt. W2544/1454 700,000 5/15 D. D. & L. A.D.S.S. Forms/C. 2118.

SECRET.

War Diary

– of the –

A.D.V.S. 30th Division

for the month of

August 1916

Volume 10

ADVS.
Vol 10

Instructions regarding War Diaries and Intelligence Summaries are contained in F. S. Regs., Part II. and the Staff Manual respectively. Title pages will be prepared in manuscript.

WAR DIARY
or
INTELLIGENCE SUMMARY.
(*Erase heading not required.*)

Army Form C. 2118.

Place	Date	Hour	Summary of Events and Information	Remarks and references to Appendices
Bray Albert Rd 7.26 d 1.1	1916 Aug 1		In Office –	
Hallencourt	" 2		Left Bray Albert Rd Head Qts at 8. am. arrived Hallencourt 7.30 P.m. Head Qtrs of Division here.	
"	" 3		Called on the D.V.S. Army. at Abbeville –	
	4		Left Hallencourt by motor bus for Longpre – Entrained at Longpre 12.54 P.m. for Berguette – arrived Berguette 7.30 P.m.	
Busnes			Left Berguette 8 P.m. arrived Divisional Hd Qts Busnes at 8.30 P.m.	
"	" 5		D.D.V.S. 1st Army called –	
"	" 6		Inspected Transport animals of 202 Field Company R.E. condition generally good.	
			Inspected " " " " " 98 Field Ambulance	
			Inspected " " " " " 16 Bn Manchester Regiment	
			Inspected " " " " " 2nd Bn Yorkshire " "	
			Attended D.D.V.S.'s conference at Head Quarters 1st Army.	
"	" 7		Inspected ~~90~~ transport animals 90th Machine Gun Company	
			" " " " 2nd Bn Royal Scot Fusiliers condition of animals	

2353 Wt. W2544/1454 700,000 5/15 D. D. & L. A.D.S.S. Forms/C. 2118.

Volume 10

Ending Aug 31. 1916

[illegible] [illegible]

CARVS.

30th [illegible]

Instructions regarding War Diaries and Intelligence Summaries are contained in F. S. Regs., Part II. and the Staff Manual respectively. Title pages will be prepared in manuscript.

WAR DIARY
or
INTELLIGENCE SUMMARY.
(Erase heading not required.)

Army Form C. 2118.

Place	Date	Hour	Summary of Events and Information	Remarks and references to Appendices
Busnes	1916 Aug 7th		Condition of animals moderate – in this respect I have seen no improvement for the past 3 months. Sent 3 horses for debility to 40 Mobile V. Section – Inspected transport animals of 201st Field Company R.E. – condition good – but saddle sore backs too frequent. Sent 3 horses for this injury to 40 M.V.S. – Inspected transport animals 17th Bn Manchester Regiment sent 1 horse to 40 M.V.S. – Inspected transport animals 18 Manchester Bn condition generally good –	
	8		Visited Haverskerque and inspected 149 Bde R.F.A. a number of debilitated cases in this Bde confined mostly to A and B batteries – when inspecting this Bde on July 31st ordered 13 horses to be sent to Mobile V Section. I am informed to day that Major Kirkland cancelled my order and these horses were not sent. Had the following horses sent to M.V.S for debility – A Battery 1. 91. 100. 38. 32. B. battery 18. 23. 53. 87. 139. 112 – C " " 82. 84. 92. 21. D. battery 47. 13. 119. 87. Visited 150 Bde condition generally good – In D. Subsection of A battery found 2 cases of mange and 5 suspicious cases – Had this section put in working isolation. Sent 2 cases of mange to M.V.S. gave instructions for suspicious cases to be clipped and treated	

Instructions regarding War Diaries and Intelligence Summaries are contained in F. S. Regs., Part II. and the Staff Manual respectively. Title pages will be prepared in manuscript.

WAR DIARY
or
INTELLIGENCE SUMMARY.
(Erase heading not required.)

Army Form C. 2118.

Place	Date	Hour	Summary of Events and Information	Remarks and references to Appendices
	1916			
BUSNES	Aug 9th		Visited Haverskerque with D.D.V.S and D.D.R 1st Army and inspected 30th Divisional Ammunition Column - Condition very good - No 4 Section not so good as No 1. 2. & 3. (for Captain F.L. Chum AVC) Received from Officer Commanding 30th D A C A.F W 3121 - for his devotion to duty and attention to units under shell fire - forwarded same to A A & Q M G. recommending same.	
"	10		Visited Haverskerque district with D.D.V.S. and D.D.R 1st Army inspecting 148. 149. 150 and 151st Bdes R.F.A.	
" "	11		Visited No 40 Mobile V. Section at St Floris.	
" "	12		Left Busnes by car at 10 am arrived Bethune 11 am.	
Bethune	13		Visited Gore and inspected 11th South Lancs condition generally good - evacuated one L D horse lame for Sandcrack	
"	14		Visited No 40 M V S at Gorre and inspected animals for evacuation - Inspected transport animals of No 3 and 4 Companies 30th Divisional Train Condition of animals very good.	
" "	15		Inspected 2nd Bn Royal Scot Fusiliers at Bethune Condition of animals generally moderate.	

Instructions regarding War Diaries and Intelligence Summaries are contained in F. S. Regs., Part II. and the Staff Manual respectively. Title pages will be prepared in manuscript.

WAR DIARY
or
INTELLIGENCE SUMMARY.
(Erase heading not required.)

Army Form C. 2118.

Place	Date	Hour	Summary of Events and Information	Remarks and references to Appendices
	1916 Aug			
Bethune	16		With D.D.V.S. and D.D.R. First Army inspecting the following units, 90th Infantry Bde. 89th Infantry Bde. 98 Field Ambulance 201 Field Co R.E. and 30th Divisional Train.	
" "	17		In Office	
"	18		Inspected horses of M.M.P. at Bethune	
			" " " 96 Field Ambulance Bethune - inspecting transport animals of 97. Field Ambulance Annezin -	
			Inspected C and D batteries 149 Bde R.F.A. (Essars)	
" "	19		Visited Gorre and inspected transport animals 2 Yorks - 2nd Wilts - 20th Kings Liverpool Regiment and 19th Manchesters also 21st Bde Machine Gun Company - 200 Field Co and 202 Field Co R.E. - also 11th - South Lancs (Pioneer Bn).	
			19 Manchesters looking on the thin side evacuated 3 animals	
			21 Bde Machine Gun Co looking light evacuated 3 animals	
" "	20		Visited No 40 Mobile V. Section at ~~Longfosse~~ Locon and inspected 26 animals for evacuation. Inspected A and B batteries 149 Bde R.F.A. evacuated several animals - These horses are improving	

Army Form C. 2118.

WAR DIARY
or
INTELLIGENCE SUMMARY.
(Erase heading not required.)

Instructions regarding War Diaries and Intelligence Summaries are contained in F. S. Regs., Part II. and the Staff Manual respectively. Title pages will be prepared in manuscript.

Place	Date	Hour	Summary of Events and Information	Remarks and references to Appendices
	1916			
Bethune	Aug 21		Visited 97 Field Ambulance Annezin - Inspected A and B batteries 148 Bde R F A Champs de Mars.	
"	22		Inspected transport animals 2nd Bn Royal Scot Fusiliers " " " " 97 Field Ambulance Annezin some of the riding horses on the thin side - Inspected A and C batteries 150 Bde R.F.A ~~Essars~~ Essars	
"	23		Inspected 17th Manchester Bn Champ de Mars - 98 Field Ambulance at Mesplaux. Visited Hd Qrs [illegible] for the purpose of inspecting the watering arrangements for horses - also D and B batteries 150 Bde R F A Essars and A B & D batteries 149 Bde R F A	
"	24		Inspected the watering arrangements for the 30th Divisional Ammunition Column - 97 Field Ambulance	
"	25		Inspecting the watering arrangements of B and C Batteries 151st Bde R F A Visited 1/1 HQ Mobile V Section Locon and inspected horses for evacuation	
"	26		Visited 1/1 HQ Mobile V Section Locon. Inspected watering arrangements of A battery 151 Bde R F A	
"	27		Visited Gorre and inspected transport animals of 200 and 202 Field Companies R.E. also 11 South Lancs - Inspected 90th Machine Gun Company Transport at Essars 2nd Royal Scot Fusiliers at Bethune - 19th Manchesters at Hinges. This unit has some mules in very light condition - 18th Liverpools at La Pannerie several animals on the light side	

Instructions regarding War Diaries and Intelligence Summaries are contained in F. S. Regs., Part II. and the Staff Manual respectively. Title pages will be prepared in manuscript.

WAR DIARY
or
INTELLIGENCE SUMMARY.
(Erase heading not required.)

Army Form C. 2118.

Place	Date	Hour	Summary of Events and Information	Remarks and references to Appendices
	1916			
Bethune	Aug 28		Visited No 40 Mobile V. Section Gorre	
			Inspected the watering arrangements of 21st Infantry Bde	
" "	29		Visited Hd Qrs R.S. Bethune and inspected horses – owing to a case of Glanders being evacuated by No 40 M.V.S. on Aug 23 from these Hd Qrs – Sent a report on the watering arrangements for all the animals of the Division to Hd Qrs	
			Visited No 40 M.V.S. with D.D.V.S. 1st Army reference case of Glanders evacuated on Aug 23	
" "	30		Tested with mallein Head Quarter horses R.S.	
			Lieut A.T. Andrews T.C. reported for duty – posted to 150 Bde R.F.A.	
" "	31		Inspected ~~[illegible]~~ 149 Bde R.F.A. horses in Essars area.	
			Inspected Hd Qrs horses R.S.	

H. Welch Major
ADVS 30th Division

2353 Wt. W2544/1454 700,000 5/15 D. D. & L. A.D.S.S./Forms/C. 2118.

SECRET.

Vol 11

War Diary

-of-

A.D.V.S., 30th Division

for the month of

September 1916

Volume XI.

H. Welch.

Major

Instructions regarding War Diaries and Intelligence Summaries are contained in F. S. Regs., Part II. and the Staff Manual respectively. Title pages will be prepared in manuscript.

WAR DIARY
or
INTELLIGENCE SUMMARY.
(Erase heading not required.)

Army Form C. 2118.

Place	Date	Hour	Summary of Events and Information	Remarks and references to Appendices
	1916			
Bethune	Sept 1		Inspected A and B batteries 150th Bde R.F.A at Essars.	
" "	2		Inspected horses of A and B batteries 148 Bde R.F.A Champs-de-Mars.	
			B battery number of horses on the light side – also inspected C battery 148 —	
			Submitted a second report to Divisional Head Quarters on watering arrangements	
			for all transport animals of the Division	
" "	3		In office	
" "	4		" "	
" "	5		" "	
" "	6		Inspected horses of B and D batteries 150 Bde Essars also D 148 Bde	
	"		Captain D.R. Williamson AVC returned from leave	
" "	"		Captain Clunes AVC left for 7 days leave	
" "	7		Visited No 40 Mobile V. Section Locon and inspected	
" "	8		Inspected transport animals of 96 Field Ambulance	
" "	.		With DDVS and DDR First Army inspecting horses considered unsuitable for artillery	
" "	9		Inspected transport animals 95 Field Ambulance at Annequin	
" "			Inspected transport animals of 16. 17. 18th Manchester Battalions at [illegible] LE TOURET.	

2353 Wt. W2544/1454 700,000 5/15 D. D. & L. A.D.S.S. Forms/C. 2118.

Volume 11.
Ending September 30/1916
H. [illegible] Major
A.V.C. 30th Div

Instructions regarding War Diaries and Intelligence Summaries are contained in F. S. Regs., Part II. and the Staff Manual respectively. Title pages will be prepared in manuscript.

WAR DIARY
or
INTELLIGENCE SUMMARY.
(Erase heading not required.)

Army Form C. 2118.

Place	Date	Hour	Summary of Events and Information	Remarks and references to Appendices
	1916			
Bethune	Sept 9		Inspected transport animals of 2nd Royal Scot Fusiliers also	
	" 10		Inspected 19th Manchester Bn transport animals at Gorre this unit not looking well a number of thin animals also inspected 2nd Bn Yorks. 18th Kings Liverpool Regiment 2nd Wilts and 21st Machine G. Company.	
" "	" 11		Inspected horses of D battery 148 Bde RFA at Essars also A B C and D batteries 149 Bde B battery - a number of thin animals - this battery condition of animals only fair -	
" "	12		Inspected A battery horses 150 Bde near Essars some 30 animals on the light side	
	"		" " B " " " " " " " Condition generally good.	
	"		" " A B and C batteries 148 Bde RFA Bethune - B battery has improved - still a number of ~~horses~~ horses on the light side.	
" "	13		Visited 40 Mobile Veterinary Section Gorre.	
			Called on C R A reference artillery horses of the Division	
	14		Visited Railway Station Bethune for the purpose of inspecting 40 Remounts arrived by train. Remounts generally in good in good condition.	
	15		Handed over to Captain Williams and proceeded on leave.	

Instructions regarding War Diaries and Intelligence Summaries are contained in F. S. Regs., Part II. and the Staff Manual respectively. Title Pages will be prepared in manuscript.

WAR DIARY
or
INTELLIGENCE SUMMARY
(Erase heading not required.)

Army Form C. 2118.

Place	Date	Hour	Summary of Events and Information	Remarks and references to Appendices
	1916			
BETHUNE.	15·9.		Took over duty from Major Welch.	
	16·9		Office	
	17·9		Office	
	18·9		Entrained for DOULLENS 12·50 pm.	
DOULLENS.			Arrived DOULLENS 4·30 pm.	
	19·9		Informed by A.A.Q.M.G. at 11·30 pm 40 M.V.S. would arrive 6·30 am 19th. Saw 40 M.V.S. detrained 9·50 am. O.C. reported receipt of wire ordering move 7 pm to be at LILLERS by 12 midnight, impossible to get there & caught next train. Left 5 horses for evacn from ESTAIRES next morning with N.C.O. & 2 men & handed it over to 31st Division. Reported train accident on LOCON-BETHUNE road, one man seriously injured taken to 94th Fd Amb, several horses injured one to be destroyed.	
	20·9		Inspected M.V.S. at HEM. D.D.V.S Res. Army called & gave instructions re returns.	
	21·9		Moved to VIGNACOURT.	
VIGNACOURT.	22·9		Inspected Transport 89 I.B. 17 Liverpools V.G. except one rider. 2nd Bedfords Good. 19th Liverpools Fair. 20th Liverpools not looking well, several thin horses, pointed this	

2449 Wt. W14957/M90 750,000 1/16 J.B.C. & A. Forms/C.2118/12.

Instructions regarding War Diaries and Intelligence Summaries are contained in F. S. Regs., Part II. and the Staff Manual respectively. Title Pages will be prepared in manuscript.

WAR DIARY
or
INTELLIGENCE SUMMARY
(Erase heading not required.)

Army Form C. 2118.

Place	Date	Hour	Summary of Events and Information	Remarks and references to Appendices
VIGNACOURT			out to T.O. & impressed upon him the necessity for improvement in the care of his animals.	
			M. G. Coy. in fair condition.	
" "	23.9		Office	
" "	24.9		Inspected R.A. on arrival in area, at TALMAS & PIERREGOT. 148 Bde looking well, 149 showed considerable improvement 150. A battery about a dozen thin horses, drew the attention of Batty commander to this. D Batty not looking at all well, pointed this out to Batty comdr & evacuated 3 of the worst cases. B' Echelon D.A.C. has several thin horses in B & D subsections. some of these are animals of poor conformation.	
" "	25.9		Inspected Remounts on arrival at Railhead. 4 chargers. 4 R. 2 H.D. 16 mules. condition fairly good. Sent Capt [illegible] to D.A.C. as R.A. moving to XV corps. & took over Section.	
" "	26.9		at M.V.S. & in office.	
	27.9		Inspected Transport of 21 Inf Bde at NAOURS. a few thin animals in 18th Liverpools. also a couple in 2nd Wilts remainder in fairly good condition	
	28.9		Handed over to Major Welch A.D.V.S.	
" "	28		Returned from leave. Took over from Captain Williamson acting A.D.V.S.	
" "	29		Visited Flesselles and inspected transport animals of the 16th & 18th Manchester Bns - 18th condition generally good - but some of the mules of the 16th are distinctly on the light side - and I drew the transport officers attention to this. also inspected 2 Bn Royal Scot Fusiliers - the condition of the animals of this unit is only fair - inspected 19 Bn Liverpool Regiment at Vignacourt there is room for a lot of improvement in the condition of many of the animals	

2449 Wt. W14957/M90 750,000 1/16 J.B.C. & A. Forms/C.2118/12.

Instructions regarding War Diaries and Intelligence Summaries are contained in F. S. Regs., Part II. and the Staff Manual respectively. Title Pages will be prepared in manuscript.

WAR DIARY
or
INTELLIGENCE SUMMARY
(Erase heading not required.)

Army Form C. 2118.

Place	Date	Hour	Summary of Events and Information	Remarks and references to Appendices
Vignacourt	Sept 1-30 1916		Inspected transport animals 17th and 20th Liverpool Bns Vignacourt condition good – inspected 89th Machine Gun Company – also 2nd Bedfordshire Regiment condition with the exception of several mules and riders in the Machine G Comp'y – Inspected transport animals 97th Field Ambulance the condition of the animals generally has much improved since my last visit – Visited 40 Mobile V. Section Vignacourt	

H. Welch Major
ADVS 30th Division
2nd October 1916

2449 Wt. W14957/M90 750,000 1/16 J.B.C. & A. Forms/C.2118/12.

Secret.

Vol 12

War Diary
of A.D.V.S. 30th Division
for the Month of
October 1916

Volume ~~1~~2

Army Form C. 2118.

Instructions regarding War Diaries and Intelligence Summaries are contained in F. S. Regs., Part II. and the Staff Manual respectively. Title Pages will be prepared in manuscript.

WAR DIARY
or
INTELLIGENCE SUMMARY
(Erase heading not required.)

Place	Date	Hour	Summary of Events and Information	Remarks and references to Appendices
Vignacourt	Oct 1 1916		Visited Warques and Naours - and inspected the transport animals of the following units - 19th Manchester Bn - 2 York Regiment 2nd Bedfordshire Bn Wiltshire Regiment - 18th Bn Liverpool Regiment also 21st Machine Gun Company. The 19th Manchester and 2nd Wilts show improvement - but there are still a number of animals on the light side.	
" "	2		In Office	
" "	3		In Office.	
" "	4		Left Vignacourt 9.30 am with Head Quarters of the Division for Buire - Arrived Buire 12.30 P.m.	
Buire	"			
" "	5		Inspected transport animals 90th Infantry Bde and 98 Field Ambulance -	
" "	6		Inspected T. & O. Mobile V. Section Ribemont.	
" "	7		Proceeded to Mericourt Station at 5.30 am to inspect remounts arriving by train at 6 am. train did not ~~arrived~~ arrive until 12.30 midday and these were not detrained until 6.30. P.m.	
" "	8		In Office - D.D.V.S. 4th Army called -	

2449 Wt. W14957/M90 750,000 1/16 J.B.C. & A. Forms/C.2118/12.

Volume 12
Ending October 31-1916
Hewlett major
A.K.V.S. 30th [illegible]

Army Form C. 2118.

Instructions regarding War Diaries and Intelligence Summaries are contained in F. S. Regs., Part II. and the Staff Manual respectively. Title Pages will be prepared in manuscript.

WAR DIARY
or
INTELLIGENCE SUMMARY
(Erase heading not required.)

Place	Date 1916	Hour	Summary of Events and Information	Remarks and references to Appendices
Buire	Oct 9th		Inspected transport animals 89th Infantry Bde at Dernacourt	
" "	10th		Visited Montauban and Mametz and inspected the transport animals 148 Bde R.F.A. 149 Bde and 150th	
"	11th		Left Buire at 8.30 am for E 11 Central. Head Quarters of Division moved to Fricourt	
E 11 Central	12		Visited 40 Mobile Veterinary Section Fricourt and inspected animals for evacuation. Visited Montauban and inspected No 1 Section 30th DAC also B battery 148 Bde R.F.A	
" "	13		Visited Mametz and Montauban. Inspected 148. 149 and 150 Bde R.F.A. also No 4 section 30th DAC. Received complaints from each Bde about the watering arrangements. Inspected same and forwarded a report on the subject to Divisional Head Quarters. This condition generally of the artillery horses is not good – (excepting C battery 148 Bde and B battery 149). A battery 149 Bde is distinctly bad.	
" "	14		Proceeded to No 40 Mobile Veterinary and inspected animals for evacuation. Visited Montauban and inspected 150 Bde R.F.A.	

2449 Wt. W14957/M90 750,000 1/16 J.B.C. & A. Forms/C.2118/12.

Instructions regarding War Diaries and Intelligence Summaries are contained in F. S. Regs., Part II. and the Staff Manual respectively. Title Pages will be prepared in manuscript.

WAR DIARY
or
INTELLIGENCE SUMMARY
(Erase heading not required.)

Army Form C. 2118.

Place	Date	Hour	Summary of Events and Information	Remarks and references to Appendices
E 11 Central	Oct 14		Inspected No 2 and 4 Companies 30th Divisional Train at E 11. Central.	
" "	" 15		Wrote to H^d Q^{trs} Division reporting regarding the watering arrangements for horses at the Meaulte[?] trough overcrowding and congestion and congestion - accommodation and supply of water inadequate for the very large number of horses watering here.	
" "	16		In office.	
" "	17		Left at 9.15 am to attend a conference at D.D.V.S.' office 4th Army - returned at 3.30 - Proceeded to Albert Station at 4.00 to inspect remounts arriving by train - Train did not arrive until 9.30 pm detrained at 10.20 pm - It is useless proceeding to Railhead to inspect animals owing to the congestion of traffic the trains arrive very late - and it is generally dark before the animals are detrained - and it is impossible to carry out any inspection - On a previous occasion I spent 14 hours waiting for the Remount train - and then was unable to inspect the animals - apart from this it considerably interferes with my other duties - and I consider it is a better arrangement to have Remounts inspected when they are posted to units.	

2449 Wt. W14957/M90 750,000 1/16 J.B.C. & A. Forms/C.2118/12.

Army Form C. 2118.

Instructions regarding War Diaries and Intelligence Summaries are contained in F. S. Regs., Part II. and the Staff Manual respectively. Title Pages will be prepared in manuscript.

WAR DIARY
or
INTELLIGENCE SUMMARY
(Erase heading not required.)

Place	Date	Hour	Summary of Events and Information	Remarks and references to Appendices
Fricourt Chateau	Oct. 18th /16		Left E 11 Central at 3 P.m. for Head Quarters of Division at Fricourt Chateau – Office and clerk arrived 10.30 P.m.	
" "	19		In Office	
" "	20		Inspected 149 and 150 Bdes R.F.A. at S.21.d. – Visited 40 M.V.S. at F.4.d.1.4. and inspected animals for evacuation.	
" "	21		Visited No 1 Company 30th Divisional Train at E.12. Central – Called on DADOS. reference Horse Rugs and clipping machines.	
" "	22		Left Fricourt Chateau at 9.30 Am. arrived Ribemont 11 Am.	
Ribemont	23		Inspected transport animals of 16th 17th 18th Manchesters also 2nd Bn Royal Scot Fusiliers and 90th Machine Gun Comp'y – animals generally looking fairly well –	
" "	24		Inspected transport animals of 96 Field Ambulance at Buire. 98 at Ribemont. also 201st Field Co – Ribemont	
" "	25		In Office –	

2449 Wt. W14957/M90 750,000 1/16 J.B.C. & A. Forms/C.2118/12.

Instructions regarding War Diaries and Intelligence Summaries are contained in F. S. Regs., Part II. and the Staff Manual respectively. Title Pages will be prepared in manuscript.

WAR DIARY
or
INTELLIGENCE SUMMARY

(Erase heading not required.)

Army Form C. 2118.

Place	Date	Hour	Summary of Events and Information	Remarks and references to Appendices
Ribemont	Oct. 26th		Head Quarters Division moved to Pas. Left Ribemont 1 P.m. Arrived PAS. 3 P.m.	
PAS.	27th		Applied for Car to visit Units – Car not available –	
"	28		Visited Bavincourt for the purpose of seeing ADVS. 46th Division to arrange to take over Office and billet. also site of Mobile V. Section.	
"	29th		In Office.	
"	30		Visited No 40 Mobile Veterinary Section at Halloy.	
Bavincourt	31		Left Pas. with Head Quarters Division at 9 am. arrived Bavincourt 10 15 am. Inspected transport animals Head Quarters Divisional Signals.	
			H C Welch Major. ADVS. 30th Division	

2449 Wt. W14957/M90 750,000 1/16 J.B.C. & A. Forms/C.2118/12.

Secret

War Diary

of

A.D.V.S. 30th Divn

for the month of

November 1916

Volume XIII

Army Form C. 2118.

Instructions regarding War Diaries and Intelligence Summaries are contained in F. S. Regs., Part II. and the Staff Manual respectively. Title Pages will be prepared in manuscript.

WAR DIARY
or
INTELLIGENCE SUMMARY
(Erase heading not required.)

Place	Date	Hour	Summary of Events and Information	Remarks and references to Appendices
Bavincourt	1.11.16		Visited U.26 a. to inspect mange bath in course of construction. Visited No 40. Mobile Veterinary Section at Sabret.	
" "	2.11.16		Visited Baillemont and inspected transport of animals of 21st Infantry Bde – 2. Yorks – 2nd Wilts – 19th Manchesters and 18th Kings Liverpool Regiment – 2nd Wilts. the condition of the animals generally is only fair – a number of L.D. are apparently on the light side – Inspected transport animals of 202 Co R.E. and 21st Machine Gun Company.	
" "	3.11		Visited and inspected transport animals 1, 2 and 4 Sections – 27th Reserve Park at Beaudricourt.	
" "	4.11		Visited 40 Mobile Veterinary Section at Sarbret – D.D.V.S. 3rd Army called – Visited and inspected transport animals of 97 Field Ambulance at La Herliere – also 200 and 201 Field Companies R.E. – Inspected 6 animals of 2nd Wilts 18th at 40 M.V.S. for examination – found two of them suffering from skin disease (suspect mange).	
" "	5.11		Visited Baillemont and inspected transport animals of 2nd Wilts – gave instructions for all animals to be clipped owing to 2 suspected cases of mange being received by 40 M.V.S. from this unit.	

2449 Wt. W14957/M90 750,000 1/16 J.B.C. & A. Forms/C.2118/12.

Volume 13

Ending

November 30 1916

H [illegible]

Major

[illegible]

30th [illegible]

Instructions regarding War Diaries and Intelligence Summaries are contained in F. S. Regs., Part II. and the Staff Manual respectively. Title Pages will be prepared in manuscript.

WAR DIARY
or
INTELLIGENCE SUMMARY
(Erase heading not required.)

Army Form C. 2118.

Place	Date	Hour	Summary of Events and Information	Remarks and references to Appendices
Bavincourt	6.11.16		Visited No 40 M.V.S. at Sarton, and inspected animals for evacuation.	
			Visited Basseux Farm and inspected transport animals of 89th Infantry Bde viz 17th - 19th and 20th Liverpools, and 2nd Bedfordshire Regiment – also 89th Machine Gun Company. In the 20th Liverpools some animals distinctly light in condition.	
" "	7.11		Visited No 40 Mobile Veterinary Section –	
" "	8.11		Visited Courcelles, and inspected transport animals of 96 and 98 Field Ambulances. also standings – watering arrangements – and Veterinary Equipment.	
" "	9.11		Visited No 1 Section 27 Reserve Park Bavincourt – condition of animals generally good –	
			Interviewed Sergeant Jennings AVC 27th Reserve Park and Q.M.S. Watson Head Quarters VII Corps – with reference to report asked for on these N.C.Os. Visited No 40 Mobile Veterinary Section and inspected animals for evacuation.	
" "	10.11		Visited La Cauchie and inspected transport animals of 11th South Lancs. sent 6 animals to 40 M.V.S. for lameness and debility – also inspected A B C and D Batteries 232 Bde R.F.A. 46th Division ——	

Instructions regarding War Diaries and Intelligence Summaries are contained in F. S. Regs., Part II. and the Staff Manual respectively. Title Pages will be prepared in manuscript.

WAR DIARY
or
INTELLIGENCE SUMMARY
(Erase heading not required.)

Army Form C. 2118.

Place	Date	Hour	Summary of Events and Information	Remarks and references to Appendices
	1916			
Bavincourt	11th November		Visited Saulty and inspected transport animals of No 1 and 3 Sections 46 DAC - also No 2 Section at Coullemont and No 514 Howitzer Battery in the same village - recently arrived from England - made arrangements to have all these animals tested with mallein -	
" "	12th		Visited No 40 M. V. S. and inspected animals for evacuation. -	
" "	13		Visited 40 Mobile Veterinary Section - Larbret. Captain Williamson left for England on 10 days special leave.	
" "	14		Inspected A B and C batteries 230 Bde R F A 46th Division at Bavincourt - Inspected transport animals of 46th Divisional Signals " " " Visited 40 Mobile Veterinary Section at Larbret - saw two bad cases of Ringworm sent in by V.O. of 232 Bde R F A (Captain Shawcross) wrote this officer calling his attention to this - and the condition these animals were sent in -	
" "	15		Visited 40 M.V.S. Larbret and inspected animals for evacuation. Inspected 2 and 4 Companies 30th Divisional Train at Larbret - Inspected the animals of Head Quarters and M.M.P. Visited La Herlière and inspected A battery 231. Bde R.F.A. Forwarded the sum of £11. 3. 0 subscriptions collected from N.C.O.s officers and men of the A.V.C. towards the Kitchener Memorial Fund - To D.D.V.S. 3rd Army -	

2449 Wt. W14957/M90 750,000 1/16 J.B.C. & A. Forms/C.2118/12.

Instructions regarding War Diaries and Intelligence Summaries are contained in F. S. Regs., Part II. and the Staff Manual respectively. Title Pages will be prepared in manuscript.

WAR DIARY
or
INTELLIGENCE SUMMARY
(Erase heading not required.)

Army Form C. 2118.

Place	Date	Hour	Summary of Events and Information	Remarks and references to Appendices
	1916 November			
Bavincourt	16		Visited Monchet, and inspected 231 Bde R.F.A. 46th Division – also inspected C battery 150 Bde R.F.A. – late 514 Howitzer battery recently arrived from England – found case of mange in the unit C.O's charger – have same sent to 40 M.V. Section.	
" "	17		Visited No 40 M.V.S at Sarbeet	
" "	18		Visited " " " " " " and inspected animals for evacuation –	
" "	19		Visited La Cauchie – and inspected transport animals of 11th South Lancs.	
" "	20		Inspected transport animals of the 2nd Bn. 18th Kings Liverpool Regt – 21st Machine Gun Company and 202 Field Co R.E. at Bailleulmont.	
" "	21		Visited Mobile Veterinary Section	
	22		Visited Fosseux and inspected 148 – 149 Bde R.F.A. (also C battery 149) Visited Grosville and inspected A and B batteries 150 Bde R.F.A. The animals generally are not looking well – sent 50 for evacuation at once for debility – also another 50 – if some improvement is not shown – these tops and hay kept very short in some of the batteries –	

2449 Wt. W14957/M90 750,000 1/16 J.B.C. & A. Forms/C.2118/12.

Army Form C. 2118.

Instructions regarding War Diaries and Intelligence Summaries are contained in F. S. Regs., Part II. and the Staff Manual respectively. Title Pages will be prepared in manuscript.

WAR DIARY
or
INTELLIGENCE SUMMARY

(Erase heading not required.)

Place	Date	Hour	Summary of Events and Information	Remarks and references to Appendices
Barricourt	November 22		Continued – Sent report to Divisional Head Qrs reference my visit to the 30th Divisional Artillery – Copies to C.R.A. and D.D.V.S. 3rd Army.	
" "	23		Visited No 40. Mobile Veterinary Section and inspected 42 animals for evacuation. Visited [illegible] and inspected No 3 Comp 30th Divisional Train –	
" "	24		Visited No 40 Mobile Veterinary Section –	
" "	25		Visited Milly near Doullens and inspected transport animals of No 1. 2. and 3 Sections 30th D.A.C. Proceeded to Grouches and inspected D. battery 150 Bde also C battery 149 Bde at Lucheux – In D battery found 6 animals for evacuation – and 15 in C. 149 –	
" "	26		In office.	
" "	27		Visited No 40. Mobile Veterinary Section [illegible] and inspected animals for Evacuation – Visited Couturelle and inspected transport animals of 96 and 98 Field ambulance. Inspected transport animals of No 4 Section 30th D.A.C. at Barricourt.	
" "	28		Visited No 40 Mobile Veterinary Section and inspected animals for Evacuation – Visited La Bazeque Farm and inspected transport animals of 19th and 20th [illegible].	

2449 Wt. W14957/M90 750,000 1/16 J.B.C. & A. Forms/C.2118/12.

Instructions regarding War Diaries and Intelligence Summaries are contained in F. S. Regs., Part II. and the Staff Manual respectively. Title Pages will be prepared in manuscript.

WAR DIARY
or
INTELLIGENCE SUMMARY
(Erase heading not required.)

Army Form C. 2118.

ADVS 30 D
Vol 13

Place	Date	Hour	Summary of Events and Information	Remarks and references to Appendices
Bauncourt	1916 November 29th		Visited No 4 Section 30th D.A.C evacuated 5 animals for debility. Visited No 40 M.V.S. Sarlet and inspected animals for evacuation to base.	
" "	30th		Visited La Bazeque Farm and inspected transport animals of the ×2nd Bn Bedfordshire Regiment. 17th Kings Liverpool Regiment and 89th Brigade Machine Gun Company.—	
			Visited La Hurliere and inspected transport animals of 97th Field Ambulance 200- and 201. Field Companies R.E	
			Visited No 40 M.V.S. Sarlet.	

H Welch
Major
ADVS 30th Division.

2449 Wt. W14957/M90 750,000 1/16 J.B.C. & A. Forms/C.2118/12.

Secret.

War Diary

-of-

A.D.V.S. 30th Division.

for the month of

December 1916

Volume 14

Instructions regarding War Diaries and Intelligence Summaries are contained in F. S. Regs., Part II. and the Staff Manual respectively. Title Pages will be prepared in manuscript.

WAR DIARY
or
INTELLIGENCE SUMMARY
(Erase heading not required.)

Army Form C. 2118.

Place	Date	Hour	Summary of Events and Information	Remarks and references to Appendices
	1916			
Bavincourt	December 1		Visited 40 Mobile V Section - In office remainder of day	
" "	2		" " " " "	
" "	3		" " " " " and inspected animals for evacuation	
" "	4		D.D.V.S. 3rd Army called - and inspected A and B batteries ~~148~~ Bde R.F.A. at Bavincourt - B.C and D batteries 150 Bde also part of No 4 Section 30th DAC. Bavincourt. Wrote S.S.O. 30th Division - asking for a special issue of linseed cake to the artillery	
" "	5		Visited No 40 Mobile V Section - then proceeded to Gros Tison farm and inspected mange Corps clipping bath - Called at Head Quarters Q - asking on what date this division would have to take over the Corps BATH - Called on Staff Captain to arrange a programme for D.D.V.S. 3rd Army to inspect the remainder of the 30th Divisional Artillery. Wrote to D.D.V.S. 3rd Army pointing out the Artillery could not ~~obtain~~ obtain clipping machines - although indented for - and under the circumstances it was impossible to clip out animals on veterinary grounds in units where skin disease was present.	
" "	6		Visited Saulty... and inspected B 150 Bde R.F.A. Ready ... - they lacks ... and have rugs very short - informed indents had been submitted for these deficiencies - The condition of this unit is only fair many animals on the poor side - there	

Volume 14

H C Welch Maj.

ADVS 30th Division

Month Ending December 1916

Army Form C. 2118.

WAR DIARY
or
INTELLIGENCE SUMMARY
(Erase heading not required.)

Instructions regarding War Diaries and Intelligence Summaries are contained in F. S. Regs., Part II. and the Staff Manual respectively. Title Pages will be prepared in manuscript.

Place	Date	Hour	Summary of Events and Information	Remarks and references to Appendices
Bavincourt	Dec 6		cannot be evacuated as this battery is now 31 animals short of its establishment.	
			Called on the Staff Captain 30th Artillery for the purpose of arranging programme for D.D.V.S. 3rd Army inspection on the 7 December.	
" "	7		D.D.V.S. 3rd Army called at 10.15 am – proceeded with him and inspected the animals of the following units 149 Bde R.F.A. at La Cauchie – A battery 148 and B. battery 150 Bde at La Herlière also Nos 1 and 3 Sections 30th DAC at Saulty.	
" "	8		Interviewed all V.O's of Division at my office and went into the matter of sore backs – due to carrying ammunition – also to cases of skin disease arising from mud – also the treatment of same – Visited 40 M.V.S. at Larbret and inspected animals for evacuation to Base.	
" "	9		Visited D battery 148 Bde R.F.A. Bavincourt and inspected transport animals of this unit – condition generally satisfactory – Hay nets and nose bags incomplete – Visited No 40 M.V.S. Larbret –	

Instructions regarding War Diaries and Intelligence Summaries are contained in F. S. Regs., Part II. and the Staff Manual respectively. Title Pages will be prepared in manuscript.

WAR DIARY
or
INTELLIGENCE SUMMARY
(Erase heading not required.)

Army Form C. 2118.

Place	Date 1916	Hour	Summary of Events and Information	Remarks and references to Appendices
Barricourt	Dec 10		Visited Coullemont and inspected ammunition column horses of C.150 Bde R.F.A. late 514 Howitzer battery which arrived from England about a month ago. Some 15 of these animals are suffering from Ringworm. Also several cases of debility. Left instructions with the Veterinary Officer i/c to send them to No 40 Mobile Veterinary Section.	
"	11		Visited ~~Laherliere~~ Laherliere and inspected B. battery 150 Bde R.F.A. Sent 4 horses to No 40. M. V. S. for debility. Also inspected A. battery 148 Bde R.F.A. in the same village. Wrote to D.D.R. 3rd Army asking when Remounts were likely to arrive for the 30th D.A.C. and Artillery as owing to their shortage in animals there were still a number of cases for evacuation for debility which I could not send away until fresh animals arrived. Visited No 40 Mobile Veterinary Section Sabot, and inspected animals for evacuation to base.	
"	12		In office	
"	13		Inspected ~~A~~ B. and C. batteries 148 Bde R.F.A. Barricourt and A battery Laherliere. B battery unsatisfactory some 20	

2449 Wt. W14957/M90 750,000 1/16 J.B.C. & A. Forms/C.2118/12.

Instructions regarding War Diaries and Intelligence Summaries are contained in F. S. Regs., Part II. and the Staff Manual respectively. Title Pages will be prepared in manuscript.

WAR DIARY
or
INTELLIGENCE SUMMARY
(Erase heading not required.)

Army Form C. 2118.

Place	Date	Hour	Summary of Events and Information	Remarks and references to Appendices
Barincourt	1916 Dec 13		Some 20 animals on the thin side - also evacuated to 40 M.V.S 8 horses for debility -	
			C Battery satisfactory very few poor ones.	
			A Battery fair 16 animals on the thin side. Evacuating [illegible] & debility cases.	
			Called on the C.R.A informing him of the unsatisfactory condition of some of the horses especially B 148 and No 4 Section 30th D.A.C	
"	" 14		Inspected A C and D batteries 150 Bde R.F.A near Barincourt. Sent 8 horses from A battery to No 40 M.V.S. for debility. C 3 and D 3. Inspected B battery 150 Bde at Saleux. Sent 4 horses to M.V.S for debility -	
			Received instructions from D.A.Q.M.G. to take over Corps dipping bath at Le Gros Tison Ferme for one week from the 16th inst. Pte Softhouse A.D.V.S clerk proceeded to England on 10 days leave.	
"	" 15		Visited La Cauchie and inspected 149 Bde R.F.A -	
			A battery has a number of thin animals. Sent 4 to M.V.S. for debility	
			B " " satisfactory very few poor.	
			C " " unsatisfactory a number of thin animals sent 6 to M.V.S. including 1 case of mange. D 149 condition satisfactory sent two cases to M.V.S	
			Captain Instone A.V.C. reported for duty from leave.	

Army Form C. 2118.

Instructions regarding War Diaries and Intelligence Summaries are contained in F. S. Regs., Part II. and the Staff Manual respectively. Title Pages will be prepared in manuscript.

WAR DIARY
or
INTELLIGENCE SUMMARY
(Erase heading not required.)

Place	Date	Hour	Summary of Events and Information	Remarks and references to Appendices
Bauncourt	Dec 15		Received instructions from Divisional H^d Q^trs at 2.30 P.m on the on the 14th to take over the VII Corps dipping Bath at Le Gros Tison Ferme on the 16th inst for one week – at the same time asking me to submit a programme of the number of horses that require dipping. Said to point out this is insufficient notice. I do not know if the Bath is in working order or will or without staff	
" "	16		Visited Corps dipping Bath	
" "	17		" " " " met D.D.V.S. 3rd Army there by appointment	
" "	18		Visited Corps dipping Bath twice	
" "	19		Proceeded on 10 days leave to England handed over office etc to Captain Williams AVC	

H Welch Maj.
ADVS 30 Divn

2449 Wt. W14957/M90 750,000 1/16 J.B.C. & A. Forms/C.2118/12.

Instructions regarding War Diaries and Intelligence Summaries are contained in F. S. Regs., Part II. and the Staff Manual respectively. Title Pages will be prepared in manuscript.

WAR DIARY
or
INTELLIGENCE SUMMARY
(Erase heading not required.)

Army Form C. 2118.

ADVS 30 D
Vol 14

Place	Date	Hour	Summary of Events and Information	Remarks and references to Appendices
	1916			
BAVINCOURT.	20.XII		Major Welch proceeded on leave, took over duties of A.D.V.S.	
	20 — 25.XII		at M.V.S. and in office. visited dipping Bath on 20th & 22nd.	
	26.XII		Inspected horses of A 148 – Gen Condn: fair. B 148 gen condn fairly good. C & D 148 good.	
	27.XII		Inspected horses of A 150 condn v. poor. no standings or covers sent 7 to M.V.S. C 150 – fair – sent 4 – D 150 – – few standings no covers – 4 –	
	28.XII		Inspected 90th Inf Bde. condn good as a whole, saw one suspicious skin case — 2nd Bn R.S. Fus. ordered clipping isolation & observation.	
	29.XII		Inspected B.150. condn fair sent 10 to M.V.S. Furnished report to D.D.V.S. Third Army on standings 669 animals no head covers no standings 260 with standings no head covers 313 head covers & no standings.	
	30.XII		at M.V.S.	
	31.XII		Inspected 21st Inf Bde except 18th K.L.R. 5 suspicious skin cases in 2nd Wilts hunted out by V.O. ordered evacuation for mange, ordered thorough examination of remainder, isoln & disinfection 3 cases suspicious skin in 19th Manch. dealt with in same way. Major Welch returned from leave & handed over to him.	

D.R. Williamson Capt AVC.
a/ADVS. 30th Div.

2449 Wt. W14957/M90 750,000 1/16 J.B.C. & A. Forms/C.2118/12.

Secret.

War Diary

-of-

A.D.V.S. 30th Division

for the month of

January 1917.

Volume 15

Instructions regarding War Diaries and Intelligence Summaries are contained in F. S. Regs., Part II. and the Staff Manual respectively. Title pages will be prepared in manuscript.

WAR DIARY
or
INTELLIGENCE SUMMARY.
(Erase heading not required.)

Army Form C. 2118.

Vol 15

A. D. V. S. 30th Division Vol XV

Place	Date	Hour	Summary of Events and Information	Remarks and references to Appendices
	1917			
BAVINCOURT.	1-I.		Handed over to Major Welch AVC on his return from leave.	
	2.I		Major Welch inspected transport 2nd Wilts and in two further cases of mange. Reported 17 cases of mange to D.D.V.S.	
	3 I		Major Welch ill, assisted in office	
	4.I.		Inspected 150th Bde R.F.A. except 'B' Batty	
	5.I.		Major Welch sent to Field Ambulance, took over duty.	
	6 I.		Office & M.V.S. Furnished special report called for by D.D.V.S. re 150th Bde R.F.A.	
	7.I.		Moved to Lucheux, interviewed C.R.A. 49th Divn. re mange in this area.	
	8 I.		Inspected 'A' 'B' 'D' 246 Bde R.F.A.	
	9 I		Visited M.V.S. 49th Divn at LE MARAIS SEC. Filthy place for M.V.S. accommodation bad, horses in field up to hocks in mud.	
	10 I.		Visited IVERGNY, & on suitable place for M.V.S. examined two cases mange at COULLEMONT on premises of Mme Lobel & advised Q. to have the premises & those of M Boutringham placed out of bounds. Notified maire & French mission.	
	11. I		Advised Q. to place standings of 'A' & 'B' 246 out of bounds. Visited LUCHEUX & found billet for M.V.S. in old mill	
	12. I		In office.	

A5834 Wt W4973/M687 750,000 8/16 D. D. & L. Ltd. Forms/C.2118/13.

Army Form C. 2118.

Instructions regarding War Diaries and Intelligence Summaries are contained in F. S. Regs., Part II. and the Staff Manual respectively. Title pages will be prepared in manuscript.

WAR DIARY
or
INTELLIGENCE SUMMARY.
(Erase heading not required.)

A.D.V.S. 30th Div vol XV.

Place	Date 1917	Hour	Summary of Events and Information	Remarks and references to Appendices
LUCHEUX	13. I		D.D.V.S. inspected B 246 ordered all remainder of animals to M.V.S. telephoned later that only definitely affected animals should be sent down.	
	14. I.		Inspected 93 skin cases at M.V.S. 49th Div returned 49th units reported action D.D.V.S.	
	15. I.		Visited SUS ST LEGER. ref mange in 3rd (WR) Field Amb, horses of 98th Fd Amb in these ordered vacation disinfection & dressing of animals, visited infected lines at MILLY & saw that notice boards were up.	
	16 I		M.V.S. arrived from L'ARBRET. had to go out & arrange with D.A.C. ref old mill as Town Major had allowed D.A.C. to occupy it.	
	17. I		Took over command M.V.S. inspected water troughs 'C' 148 Bde infected with mange ordered them to M.V.S. for disinfection & procured 2 new from R.E. for this Unit.	
	18. I.		Reported Q. 9 strays collected at GROUCHES. one with mange.	
	19. I.		Interviewed D.A.D.O.S. re clippers, records supply of & quick weary of.	
			Advised 'Q' place billets SUS-ST-LEGER out of bounds.	
	20. I		Inspected 149 Bde R.F.A. found considerable improvement on the whole, a mange case in 'C' on the lines	
	21. I.		Inspected 'A' 'B' 'D' 148 Bde R.F.A.	
	22 I.		Delivered lecture in Palladium LUCHEUX on MANGE, large attendance, standing room only.	
			Inspected 'C' 148 & forwarded report to CRA on the two Bdes.	
	23. I.		Visited premises of M. VEZIEZ AUGUSTE. Billet 102 LUCHEUX. found two severe cases of mange being treated by Civilian V.S. Advised Q. to place out of bounds. inspected animals at M.V.S. for evacuation.	

Instructions regarding War Diaries and Intelligence Summaries are contained in F. S. Regs., Part II. and the Staff Manual respectively. Title pages will be prepared in manuscript.

WAR DIARY
or
INTELLIGENCE SUMMARY.
(Erase heading not required.)

Army Form C. 2118.

A.D.V.S. 30th Division Vol XV

Place	Date 1917	Hour	Summary of Events and Information	Remarks and references to Appendices
LUCHEUX.	24. I		At M.V.S. signed Evacn rolls labels &c. accompanied animals to Railhead.	
			Reported D.D.V.S. suspected case, Ulcerative Cellulitis & asked for instructions as to disposal.	
			Inspected infected premises GROUCHES, BOUT DES PRÈS, MILLY	
	25. I		Inspected infected premises LUCHEUX & reported result to G.	
	26. I		Attended conference D.D.V.S. office ST. POL.	
	27. I		D.D.V.S. inspected M.V.S saw the case of Ulc Cellulitis & confirmed diagnosis.	
	28. I		2 Coys R.E. & 1 Coy XI S Lancs to forward area notified A.D.V.S. 14th Div.	
	29. I		Notified A.D.V.S. 14th that R.A. moved to his area 30 & 31st.	
	30. I		Capt Hobbs reported fit for duty from staff, directed him to proceed 150 A.F.A. Bde for duty & report A.D.V.S. 49th Div.	
	31. I		Inspected 21st Inf Bde & 89th Inf Bde, 96th & 97th Fd Ambs.	
			H.Q. of Both Bdes poor especially 89th no rugs for mules, shivering with cold.	
			Supervision by T.O.s bad only saw two during whole inspection.	
			Reported Road GRENAS to MONDICOURT strewn with nails, to G.	

D H Williamson Capt AVC
a/A.D.V.S. 30th Division

A5834 Wt. W4973/M687 750,000 8/16 D. D. & L. Ltd. Forms/C.2118/13

Secret

War Diary

of

A.D.V.S. 50th Division

for the Month of

February 1917

Volume 16

Instructions regarding War Diaries and Intelligence Summaries are contained in F. S. Regs., Part II. and the Staff Manual respectively. Title pages will be prepared in manuscript.

WAR DIARY
or
~~INTELLIGENCE SUMMARY.~~
(Erase heading not required.)

Army Form C. 2118.

ADVS XVI 30 D
Vol 16

Place	Date	Hour	Summary of Events and Information	Remarks and references to Appendices
LUCHEUX	5.2.17	after noon	Took over duties of ADVS. 30th Division from Capt WILLIAMSON AVC who was acting since evacuation of Major WELCH AVC. Visited 40th M.V.S. saw 70 cases of sick horses under treatment & awaiting evacuation. Congestion owing to Railway traffic for evacuation of sick horses being suspended.	
"	6.2.17	9am	Divisional HQ moved to BERNEVILLE & 40th MVS to LARBRET (about 6 miles from DHQ)	
BERNEVILLE	7.2.17		Reported move of Divisional HQ & MVS to DDVS. Received notice that Railway traffic for evacuation of sick animals was reopened horses to be evacuated once a week WEDNESDAY for the AUBIGNY - ST.POL line & THURSDAY for SAULTY - DOULLENS line. In case of a move, it is arranged between OC MVS & RTO's for special arrangements to be made. Visited 40th MVS & saw horses for evacuation. O.C. M.V.S. notified of above evacuation arrangements. ~~[illegible]~~ Notified DDVS. re units left behind, for necessary veterinary attendance	
"	8.2.17		M.V.S evacuated 31 sick today, including 13 cases of Mange & 1 Ulcerative Cellulitis.	
"	9.2.17		Inspected 148th Bde RFA & Transport of 21st Inf. Bde at BEAUMETZ, on the whole the horses were looking well; except for a few in D Bty 257 which I ordered to be evacuated for Debility. Nearly all horses are under cover. Saw 1 case Mange in 2nd WILTS & ordered it to MVS at once.	
"	10.2.17		Visited MVS & saw a case of Ulcerative Cellulitis in a horse from "A" Bty 149 Bde RFA. Reported this to DDVS. All precautions to prevent spread taken.	

A5834 Wt W4973/M687 750,000 8/16 D. D. & L. Ltd. Forms/C2118/13

Instructions regarding War Diaries and Intelligence Summaries are contained in F. S. Regs., Part II. and the Staff Manual respectively. Title pages will be prepared in manuscript.

WAR DIARY
or
~~INTELLIGENCE~~ SUMMARY.
(Erase heading not required.)

Army Form C. 2118.

Place	Date	Hour	Summary of Events and Information	Remarks and references to Appendices
BERNEVILLE	10.2.17 (cont)		Arranged with OC. MVS to have all cases for evacuation sent into MVS on Tuesdays for despatch to L of C on Thursdays. Except urgent cases & cases of Contagious & Infectious Disease etc.	
" "	11.2.17.		Visited transport lines of 89th Bde with Lieut Andrew AVC. Examined two mules of 11th Bn. S. Lancs for transfer to 2nd WILTS, both animals serviceable, one rather old the other rather poor.	
" "	12.2.17		Visited lines of CRA & CRE. Went BEAUMETZ & saw transport of 2nd WILTS. ref case of MANGE.	
" "	13.2.17.		Went MONCHIET & inspected horses of 149th Bde R.F.A. & 89th Infy Bde. Artillery horses on whole looking well, big percentage infected with lice. About 50 horses in the brigade are thin and are picketed on separate lines, & having extra diet. Infy transport fairly good condition. In afternoon visited 200th 201st, 202nd F Coy RE. all animals looking very well. Saw a case of Ulcerative Cellulites in "A" Bty 149 Bde. instructed V.O to send it to MVS for evacuation.	
" "	14.2.17		Visited horse lines of C.R.A, CRE, Signals, & HQ. Motored to M.V.S. & inspected animals for evacuation on 15th inst. Saw 3 cases of Ulcerative Cellulitis 2 from A Bty 149 Bde RFA 1 from 27th Reserve Park.	
" "	15.2.17		Went to MONDICOURT & saw 97th Fd Ambulance. Also to HALLOY & saw horses of 3rd Labour Bn. Inspected animals of 148th Bde RFA & 21st Infy Bde at BEAUMETZ in the forenoon. All animals looking fairly well on whole, about 25 thin horses in RFA Bde.	

A5834 Wt. W4973/M687 750,000 8/16 D. D. & L. Ltd. Forms/C.2118/13.

Army Form C. 2118.

Instructions regarding War Diaries and Intelligence Summaries are contained in F. S. Regs., Part II. and the Staff Manual respectively. Title pages will be prepared in manuscript.

WAR DIARY
or
INTELLIGENCE SUMMARY.
(Erase heading not required.)

Place	Date	Hour	Summary of Events and Information	Remarks and references to Appendices
BERNEVILLE	15.2.17	(cont).	In afternoon visited lines of 30th DAC A & B Echelons, all animals looking well. Saw 2 Mange cases which had been isolated by V.O i/c, instructed him to send them to MVS for evacuation.	
			Received orders for posting of Lt P.J. O'BRIEN AVC (TC) on his arrival to 232 AFA Bde.	
			DDVS ordered a V.O of the division to take over veterinary charge of No 1 Sect 27 Reserve Park at GOMBREMETZ; Capt METIVIER AVC detailed.	
" "	16.2.17		V.O's attended office & brought their weekly returns.	
" "	17.2.17		Saw 3 suspected Mange cases in 149 Bde R.F.A with V.O i/c. Sent one to M.V.S & order the other two to be kept under observation & in isolation.	
			Visited 30th Div Train with V.O i/c & went round all the animals. All looking very well. Went to M.V.S & saw 5 Mange cases from 27th Reserve Park.	
			Received report from CAPT METIVIER V.O i/c 27th Reserve Park re the horses of this unit being poor & above cases of Mange. Arranged to inspect unit tomorrow.	
			CAPT CHALK AVC & Lt P.J. O.BRIEN AVC reported arrival at M.V.S last night. 1 posted to 30th DAC & 1 to 232 AFA BDE.	
			Saw DAQMG reference getting extra rations for 148 & 149 Bdes R.F.A & am sending an official report asking for the extra food.	

A5831 Wt. W4973/M687 750,000 8/16 D. D. & L. Ltd. Forms/C.2118/13.

Army Form C. 2118.

WAR DIARY
or
~~INTELLIGENCE SUMMARY.~~
(Erase heading not required.)

Instructions regarding War Diaries and Intelligence Summaries are contained in F. S. Regs., Part II. and the Staff Manual respectively. Title pages will be prepared in manuscript.

Place	Date	Hour	Summary of Events and Information	Remarks and references to Appendices
BERNEVILLE	18.2.17		Visited M.V.S. & saw cases for evacuation	
			Went with CAPT METIVIER AVC. & inspected No I Sect 27th Reserve Park. Found 7 cases Mange & 7 very suspicious cases of same. On whole horses not in a satisfactory condition. All being clipped out, most of them infested with lice.	
			Reported these Mange cases to DDVS by phone & arranged to meet him at 10.30 am tomorrow to inspect this Unit.	
" "	19.2.17		Met DDVS at MVS & he inspected Mange Cases from No I Sect 27 Reserve Park & DAC (38th Div)	
			Went on to No I Sect 27th Reserve Park & inspected unit. Found 8 Mange, 4 Suspicious, 6 animals for isolation & observation, 3 Debility. Evacuated 8 Mange & 3 Debility.	
			Sent detailed report on above to D.D.V.S.	
" "	20.2.17		Indented for canvas suits for M.V.S & 6 blow-lamps for disinfection purposes.	
			Met CAPT METIVIER AVC & went by car with ADMS to NORTH IRISH HORSE, saw their sick & contacts of Mange case, latter no appearance of infection, & had been isolated 3 weeks.	
" "	21.2.17		Received information from Q that the Dipping Bath at LE GROS TISON FARM would be at our disposal after 2.30 pm 23rd inst; & suggesting that some of the animals of 90th Infy Bde should be dipped as the bath is long way from this area & horses are working hard in this area.	
			Wired ADVS 58th DIV (& 90th Infy Bde) asking for approximate numbers of clipped horses from 90th Bde for clipping; also all V.Os for numbers of Mange contacts for dipping.	
" "	22.2.17		Saw Q reference sending animals to Dipping Bath, found advisable to only send from 90th Bde, as roads stopped for all traffic in that direction & also units working hard with horses.	

A5834 Wt W4973/M687 750,000 8/16 D. D. & L. Ltd. Forms/C.2118/13.

Instructions regarding War Diaries and Intelligence Summaries are contained in F. S. Regs., Part II. and the Staff Manual respectively. Title pages will be prepared in manuscript.

WAR DIARY
or
INTELLIGENCE SUMMARY.
(Erase heading not required.)

Army Form C. 2118.

Place	Date	Hour	Summary of Events and Information	Remarks and references to Appendices
BERNEVILLE	22.2.17	(cont).	Went DAC & saw 12 cases of suspected Mange, gave instructions for them to be clipped & kept under observation.	
" "	23.2.17		T.O's came to office with weekly returns. 90th Infy Bde sent animals to dipping bath at LE GROS TISON FARM.	
			Went to 149 R.F.A. Bde & saw suspicious skin case, but appeared to be MUD RASH, ordered isolation & observation.	
			Remounts to arrive Railhead at 8pm, so no good going to inspect them. Asked Q for list, so as to see them in their Units.	
" "	24.2.17		207 horses sent through the dipping bath.	
			Wrote DDVS asking permission to disinfect a horse billet at MONCHIET, which was labelled MANGE; it is a good building all brick & amenable to disinfection	
" "	25.2.17		Inspected 27th Reserve Park & sent report to DDVS. All horses looking well, except No I Section; suggested only working horses of latter unit every second day.	
" "	26.2.17		Saw Remounts of 145 149 Bde RFA. 21st Infy Bde & DAC; an excellent lot.	
" "	27.2.17		Saw isolated skin cases of 30th DAC. ordered 8 to be sent to M.V.S for evacuation.	
			Visited MONCHIET & saw Town Major re disinfecting Horse Billet No Q21 a.4.1. & occupation by a Fd Coy R.E.	
" "	28.2.17		Went to M.V.S. & saw animals for evacuation to L of C.	
			Inspected 6 Remounts of Divisional Train at LABRET.	
			Standings in M.V.S very bad, but O.C. unable to get any material for repairing them at present.	Vol XVI
			R.A. Goodall Capt AVC ADVS 30th Div.	

A5834 Wt W4973/M687 750,000 8/16 D. D. & L. Ltd. Forms/C.2118/13.

Secret

War Diary

- of -

A. D. V. S. 30th Divn

for the month of

March 1917

Volume 17.

5

Instructions regarding War Diaries and Intelligence Summaries are contained in F. S. Regs., Part II. and the Staff Manual respectively. Title pages will be prepared in manuscript.

WAR DIARY
or
~~INTELLIGENCE SUMMARY.~~
(Erase heading not required.)

Army Form C. 2118.

Place	Date	Hour	Summary of Events and Information	Remarks and references to Appendices
BERNEVILLE	1.3.17		Visited A & D Btys 149 Bde RFA. Two cases of Debility in A Bty for evacuation. Visited 2nd Wilts Transport instructed them to clip out any animals not already done, as they have had several cases of Mange. Received sanction for full ration Oats & 4 lbs extra Straw for 75 RA horses (25 in 148 Bde & 50 in 149 Bde R.F.A).	
" "	2.3.17		V.O's brought Weekly Returns to the office. Visited 96th Field Ambulance at GOUY, animals looking well; also saw No I Section DAC; two mules which had come in from detachment showed signs of itchiness & loss of hair on neck, isolated for clipping. Enquired from C.R.E for material to repair horse-lines in M.V.S. Informed I could get chalk by arrangement with Town Major of LABRET; advised O.C. 40th M.V.S.	
" "	3.3.17		Instructed O.C. M.V.S to meet Remount Train at WARLINCOURT at 3pm. Notified ADVS 49th Division that 40th M.V.S had collected a horse of his division on 1st inst & sent it to L of C (collected from LA CAUCHIE). Sent Circ: Memo to all V.O's to carefully remove hide from all carcases, salt them, & send them to 40th M.V.S.	
" "	4.3.17		Inspected Remounts of 148 Bde R.F.A at BEAUMETZ, moderate only. Visited MONCHIET & instructed LT ANDREWS AVC to do CAPT ADAMS work while he was on leave. CAPT ADAMS. AVC. went on leave. Memo from DDVS wanting MANGE cases reporting to him immediately besides Weekly Return, circulated to all V.O's.	
" "	5.3.17		Went through all files in the office & destroyed those no longer required. Received instructions from DDVS to arrange vety attendance for 2nd Suffolk Regt 3rd Division who are in our area. Found they are at GROUCHES near 90th Inf Bde (30th Div), so wrote DDVS that 58th Div VOs were nearer, but at present CAPT METNIER would attend them & render A2000.	

Army Form C. 2118.

WAR DIARY
or
~~INTELLIGENCE SUMMARY.~~
(Erase heading not required.)

Instructions regarding War Diaries and Intelligence Summaries are contained in F. S. Regs., Part II. and the Staff Manual respectively. Title pages will be prepared in manuscript.

Place	Date	Hour	Summary of Events and Information	Remarks and references to Appendices
BERNEVILLE	6.3.17		Went GOUY to see VO of 30th DAC & inspect two Suspected Skin Cases, found them still unclipped as clipping blades blunt.	
" "	7.3.17		Arranged to call in as many blunt blades as possible, for DADOS to have sharpened. Visited M.V.S. & saw cases for evacuation. Inspected 9 DAC Remounts (Mules), 2 in poor condition, 3 rather small 4 fairly good; reported same to DAQMG, as CRA had reported badly on them. Visited animals of 96th Field Ambulance, 6 cases of animals off-feed, no fever; One case suspicious of PURPUREA HAEMORRHAGICA.	
" "	8.3.17		Received an Auto-Grinder for renovating & sharpening clipping blades, from DADOS & sent to M.V.S. Visited GOMBREMETZ & inspected No I Sect. 27th Reserve Park, sent 2 to M.V.S for Mange & put 2 more on the "Observation Line" making (13) in all under observation for Skin. These animals are infected with lice, which are very difficult to remove; they are to be washed in a sol. of Acetic Acid & two days later with sol: Nicotine. All stables are going to be submitted to thorough disinfection with blow Lamp. Reported above to D.D.V.S.	
" "	9.3.17		Received instructions from DDVS for CAPT METIVIER AVC to hand over N I Horse + 27th Reserve Park to CAPT DUNLOP MARTIN VO to VII Corps Troops. VO's brought Weekly Returns to Office. Inspected A B & D Btys. 149 Bde R.F.A. at MONCHIET; A & D Btys not looking well, many thin horses. Standing require picking, levelling & ramming. Forwarded CAPT METIVIER'S name for Mention in Despatches. OC. 40th M.V.S forwarded following names through this office:- SE10532 Pte. J. HARDMAN for DCM & TU058179 Dr. H.C. MILLER for mention in dispatches.	

A5834 Wt. W4973/M687 750,000 8/16 D. D. & L. Ltd. Forms/C.2118/13.

Instructions regarding War Diaries and Intelligence Summaries are contained in F. S. Regs., Part II. and the Staff Manual respectively. Title pages will be prepared in manuscript.

WAR DIARY
or
~~INTELLIGENCE SUMMARY.~~

(Erase heading not required.)

Army Form C. 2118.

Place	Date	Hour	Summary of Events and Information	Remarks and references to Appendices
BERNEVILLE	10/3/17		Inspected "C" Bty. 149 Bde, also Transport animals of 21st Infy Bde, 200, 201, 202nd Fd Coy RE at MONCHIET. The animals of all these Units looked well; but standings are in bad condition. This was pointed out to the Officers i/c.	
" "	11/3/17		Sent V.O 9.30pm to see case of Tetanus at 17th Manchesters, they had telephoned Q for a V.O, but are under 55th Bde for vety attendance. Started in car with DADVS for M.V.S at LARBRET but got stuck in mud on ARRAS RD & had to come back without getting to M.V.S.	
" "	12/3/17		Went to M.V.S & saw 4 horses sent in by V.O i/c VII Corps H.A. all infected with lice & diagnosed as "Suspected Skin", wrote the V.O & asked him to clip & diagnose these cases in future. Report from O.C. 40 M.V.S that he had inspected a carcase of a heifer at M. DERAMCOURT. FERME St ARNAULD, which it was intended to sell for human consumption, & found it had been suffering from ANTHRAX. Diagnosed microscopically.	
" "	13/3/17		Went to FERME St ARNAULD inspected premises where the cow had been bled, instructed re reference disinfection & taking of all animals temperatures daily. M.O. for VII Corps HQ also present, he stated he would take steps to prohibit sale of butter & milk from this farm to British Troops. Sent report to MAIRE of SAULTY & advised that no butter or milk should be used from the farm until declared free of disease by veterinary officer. Reported to DDVS, APM, DADMS, & French Mission & advised that the premises should be put out of bounds for all animals for 15 days (time laid down by French Law).	
" "	14/3/17		Went round stables of Div HQ, CRA & Signals. Went MONCHIET & inspected vety equipment of 149 Bde RFA, 89th Infy Bde, Fd Coys RE. Saw Transport animals of 2nd Yorks at BEAUMETZ, 2 cases of fever simple, ordered all temperatures to be taken daily, report [illegible] [illegible] out and 15 book.	

A5834 Wt. W4973/M687 750,000 8/16 D. D. & L. Ltd. Forms/C.2118/13.

Instructions regarding War Diaries and Intelligence Summaries are contained in F. S. Regs., Part II. and the Staff Manual respectively. Title pages will be prepared in manuscript.

WAR DIARY
or
~~INTELLIGENCE SUMMARY.~~
(*Erase heading not required.*)

Army Form C. 2118.

Place	Date	Hour	Summary of Events and Information	Remarks and references to Appendices
BERNEVILLE	15/3/17		Went BEAUMETZ & inspected veterinary equipment of 148 RFA Bde & 21st Infy BDE; nearly all complete & in good condition. No sick evacuated to L of C yesterday owing to trains altered to Saturdays.	
" "	16/3/17		Inspected veterinary equipment of M.V.S & Divisional Train, all complete & in very good condition. Also saw animals for evacuation. Summary of A2000 Admitted 58. Cured 55. Died 4. Destroyed 2. (None Transferred Sick).	
" "	17/3/17		CAPT ADAMS AVC returned from leave. Inspected vety equipment of Div HQ & Signals.	
" "	18/3/17		Visited 30th DAC at new camp Map Reference Q20.d; saw one mange case & one very suspicious, both were clipped out & isolated, sent worse to M.V.S & other for observation. Also inspected DAC vety equipment, instrument in AVC Sgts wallets deficient, told VO i/c to go into the matter & make a report to me. Went BEAUMETZ & saw two cases of MANGE in DBC 148 RFA Bde. also 3 Debility cases.	
" "	20/3/17		Inspected Transport animals of 2nd WILTS REGT. Went M.V.S & then with CAPT METIVIER AVC to No 1 Secl 27 Reserve Park, inspected all animals & evacuated 1 to M.V.S for MANGE, reported to DDVS that this unit now free of MANGE. DDVS wired for this division to arrange vety attendance for VII Corps Troops; instructed CAPT METIVIER AVC to take over charge. Re-arrangement of V.O's owing to change in location of units. CAPT ADAMS placed in charge of 148 & 149 RFA Bdes. LT ANDREW 2 Infy Bdes, 3 Coys RE & 96th F. Ambulance. Wired ADVS 56th Div to take over vety charge of 21st Infy Bde vice 90th Infy Bde which has come forward.	

A5834 Wt. W4973/M687 750,000 8/16 D. D. & L. Ltd. Forms/C.2118/13.

Instructions regarding War Diaries and Intelligence Summaries are contained in F. S. Regs., Part II. and the Staff Manual respectively. Title pages will be prepared in manuscript.

WAR DIARY
or
~~INTELLIGENCE SUMMARY.~~
(Erase heading not required.)

Army Form C. 2118.

Place	Date	Hour	Summary of Events and Information	Remarks and references to Appendices
BERNEVILLE	21/3/17		Went to RFA Horse lines between WAILLY & AGNY & saw CAPT ADAMS AVC re looking after both R.F.A. Brigades. ADVS 56th DIVISION wired saying he would take over vety charge of 21st Infy Bde in back area. One case Mange evacuated from "A" Bty 149 Bde. R.F.A. DDVS' orders re burning some straw, certain articles, & disinfecting buildings at FERME St ARNAULD where Anthrax had occurred, have been carried out under supervision of OC. M.V.S.	
" "	22/3/17		Visited 30th D.A.C. & evacuated a MANGE case to M.V.S. Divisional Order published re Spare sets of horse shoes being used up every month & new ones being fitted to animals' feet & then put away to replace those used up, thus ensuring proper fitting of all spare shoes. Received D.V.S. Circ Memo re Sale of Unserviceable Animals to Bona Fide French Farmers. also " " " that loss of instruments in vety wallets etc must be replaced at the expense of V.O's concerned.	
" "	23/3/17		V.O's brought Weekly Returns to office. Received notification that 150 Bde. A.F.A. had been attached to this division. Capt ADAM AVC placed in charge as their V.O on leave.	
BRETENCOURT	24/3/17		Div HQ moved about 9am to BRETENCOURT. Inspected 3 batteries of 150 Bde. Animals poor. All RFA horses in open (fields) fairly good under foot & a little grazing to be had. Water supply good.	
" "	25/3/17		Visited No 1 Sect. DAC., sent two horses to M.V.S. for Debility. 21st Infy Bde reported that their animals were in a bad state owing to excessive work. CAPT ADAM AVC inspected them & reported that all looking fairly well, & had not lost condition during last 10 days.	
" "	26/3/17		Inspected thin animals of 149 Bde R.F.A. about 19 in all but not too poor. Rendered report re cutting down Horse Shoe Nails from usual 60 per set to HD 50. R & LD 40. Mules 36.	

A5834 Wt. W4973/M687 750,000 8/16 D. D. & L. Ltd. Forms/C.2118/13.

Vol 17

Army Form C. 2118.

ADVS 30 D

Vol 17

WAR DIARY
or
~~INTELLIGENCE SUMMARY.~~
(Erase heading not required.)

Instructions regarding War Diaries and Intelligence Summaries are contained in F. S. Regs., Part II. and the Staff Manual respectively. Title pages will be prepared in manuscript.

Place	Date	Hour	Summary of Events and Information	Remarks and references to Appendices
BRETENCOURT	27/3/17		Went to 27th Reserve Park at COULLEMONT with CAPT METIVIER AVC & inspected some thin horses that had just been transferred from another Park, some of them (3) to be evacuated to L of C. CAPT. SPARROW AVC took over No. 7th Irish Horse & 27th Reserve Park from Capt METIVIER AVC.	
" "	28/3/17		Rendered report to DDVS re Prevalence of Mange in Clipped & Unclipped Horses & Mules. Went to HQ. 30th DAC & saw a suspected case of Mange, animal showing thickening of skin, eruptions, prurigo, but with history of irritation set up by "Mud", evacuated to M.V.S for observation. Inspected A & D Bty 148 Bde also B & D Bty 150 Bde AFA with a view to picking out horses that will not stand much hard work, & to try to get Remounts to replace them, D Bty 148 had 5, A Bty 148 had 2; B Bty 150 had 11 & D Bty 150 had 16; some of these should be evacuated to L of C for Debility now, but as Btys are already under strength they cannot be spared.	
" "	29/3/17		Finished inspection of 148 RFA Bde & 150 RFA Bde. Reported to Q & DDVS that there were at least 30 horses in 150 Bde which ought to be evacuated for Debility, but cannot be spared until Remounts replace them.	
" "	30/3/17		V.O's brought Weekly Returns to Office. Went to M.V.S & inspected animals for evacuation. Many bad cases of Debility.	
" "	31/3/17		Went round 114 Heavy Bty RGA as V.O i/c was sick, evacuated 2 Mange, 12 Debility & 3 Ulcerative Cellulitis. Notified all V.O's to send sick to M.V.S any day of the week now.	

R.A. Gooderidge
Major AVC.
ADVS 30th Division

Secret

Vol 18

War Diary

-of-

A.D.V.S. 30th Divn

for the month of

April 1917

Instructions regarding War Diaries and Intelligence Summaries are contained in F. S. Regs., Part II. and the Staff Manual respectively. Title pages will be prepared in manuscript.

WAR DIARY
or
~~INTELLIGENCE SUMMARY.~~
(*Erase heading not required.*)

Army Form C. 2118.

Place	Date	Hour	Summary of Events and Information	Remarks and references to Appendices
BRETENCOURT	1/4/17		DDVS wired me to consolidate 155 Bde AFA returns with this division, past returns had to be rendered as were already despatched.	
			Went BEAUMETZ & sent away to 40th M.V.S from 114 HB RGA 12 Cases Debility & 3 of Ulcerative Cellulitis.	
" "	2/4/17		Rode to RANSART & inspected Debility cases of 155 Bde AFA, only 6 for evacuation in one Bty & 10 in another.	
" "	3/4/17		Inspected thin animals of 150 Bde AFA & 148 Bde R.F.A. 7 horses in one battery died on lines last night, & several more in other batteries, evidently owing to Debility & exposure, as very cold strong wind & snow.	
			Inspected HQ Signals & CRE animals, all looking well.	
			Received instructions from DDVS to look after VII Corps H.A (9 batteries) CAPT CHALK AVC (30th DAC) detailed; all batteries very close together.	
			Asked ADVS 56 Div to do the one battery of VII Corps HA at BEAUMETZ in his area.	
			Indented for instruments to complete Farriers Wallets, on repayment by V.Os. Nearly all deficiencies old standing, & it would be very difficult to trace person liable for their loss.	
" "	4/4/17		CAPT SHARPE AVC 155 AFA Bde evacuated sick. Notified D.D.V.S.	
			Went to MVS to see OC re establishing an Advanced Collecting Post for forthcoming operations.	
			CAPT R. WOOF AVC reported arrival from leave for duty with 150 Bde AFA.	
" "	5/4/17		Wired DDVS that CAPT SHARPE AVC evacuated to <u>BASE</u> on 3/4/17.	
			Rode to BLAIRVILLE with OC MVS to choose site for an Advanced Collecting Post for MVS. Found a suitable spot. In conjunction with AQMG, considered that ACP not necessary until RA Wagon lines move forward, & when they do, BLAIRVILLE will be a good place for the A.C.P.	

A5834 Wt. W4973/M687 750,000 8/16 D. D. & L. Ltd. Forms/C.2118/13.

Instructions regarding War Diaries and Intelligence Summaries are contained in F. S. Regs., Part II. and the Staff-Manual respectively. Title pages will be prepared in manuscript.

WAR DIARY
or
INTELLIGENCE SUMMARY.
(*Erase heading not required.*)

Army Form C. 2118.

Place	Date	Hour	Summary of Events and Information	Remarks and references to Appendices
BRETENCOURT	6/4/17		VO's brought their Weekly Returns to this office.	
			Rode to BLAIRVILLE with Lt ANDREW AVC & saw transport animals of 11th S. LANCS, they were on poor side, & informed Q that they would require 2 LD & 2 HD from Remounts as soon as possible, as these 4 would soon be evacuated for Debility.	
			Went on to GROSVILLE & saw transport animals of 98 F.A. they were in fair Condition.	
			Wrote R.S.O. SAULTY re supplying Conducting Parties with empty petrol tins, for watering horses in trucks en route for L of C Hospitals.	
" "	7/4/17		Signed & dispatched Weekly Returns. Very high wastage when 150 Bde & 155 Bde AFA included. Transferred Sick 112 – Died 59 – Destroyed 9 – but of these only 17 deaths in units belonging to 30th Dn, remainder were in attached Units.	
			Rendered a report ref this high wastage, & stated that it was due to hard work, exposure & short rations. Clipped animals suffered badly, & mules not affected.	
" "	8/4/17		Rode round 150 Bde AFA horses. Slight improvement with warmth of last two days.	
" "	9/4/17		Evacuate one case Sarcoptic Mange from A Bty 149 Bde	
			Capt METIVIER AVC moved up to BELLACOURT with 30th Dn Train HQ, & handed over 1 Troop North Irish Horse for vety attendance to OC M.V.S.	
			Offensive commenced	
" "	10/4/17		Handed over VII Corps HA to Capt PAUL AVC.	
			Rode to BOISLEUX-au-MONT to find a site for 40th M.V.S. as this is to be Divisional Railhead in a few days time. In meantime M.V.S. will establish an Advanced Collecting Post at 59a, until arrangements made for entrainment of sick horses at new railhead, when whole section will move up.	
			All Battery Wagon Lines moved forward. Put three exhausted 6 DG horses up for the night. & sent them to 56th DIVISION M.V.S. following morning.	

A5834 Wt. W4973/M687 750,000 8/16 D. D. & L. Ltd. Forms/C.2118/13.

Instructions regarding War Diaries and Intelligence Summaries are contained in F. S. Regs., Part II. and the Staff Manual respectively. Title pages will be prepared in manuscript.

WAR DIARY
or
~~INTELLIGENCE SUMMARY.~~
(Erase heading not required.)

Army Form C. 2118.

Place	Date	Hour	Summary of Events and Information	Remarks and references to Appendices
BRETENCOURT	11/4/17		Under DDVS instructions, inspected animals of 150 + 155 AFA Bdes, rendered report that they were looking poor, & required remounts to relieve the strain of present horses, as both Bdes are about 150 animals below strength.	
			Established an advanced Collecting Post M.V.S at pond 59d, near Boisleaux au Mont.	
" "			A.D.V.S. 33rd Div. took over vety charge of 150 + 155 AFA Bdes.	
			30th Div. came out of the line except the Artillery.	
" "	12/4/17		Div HQ marched to POMMIER, notified DDVS.	
POMMIER	13/4/17		Re allotted units amongst VO's, left 1 V.O with 148 + 149 Bde RFA & 1 with 30th DAC.	
			Received report from DDVS re Debility cases having died en route to L of C in the train, & others had to be destroyed, due to not being watered for 30 hrs. Arrangements have now been made to put 4 gall tins of water for each horse in the trucks for the journey.	
" "	14/4/17		Rode to 33rd Div HQ & tried to find ADVS re our artillery being attached to his division, only found M.V.S officer with whom I left a message for 33rd Div A.D.V.S. that I was withdrawing the 40th M.V.S advanced Collecting Post as his M.V.S. was close up to the Artillery.	
			Visited 40th M.V.S in afternoon.	
			DDVS telephoned at night, that 33rd Div wanted us to lend 1 NCO & 4 men to their M.V.S. I proposed that the 40th M.V.S. should furnish the conducting parties instead. DDVS wired 33rd Div to this effect.	
" "	15/4/17		Inspected Bde HQ & Regt Transport animals of 90th Infy Bde, all in very good condition except 2nd R. Scots Fusiliers, which were poor.	
			Rode to M.V.S in afternoon & saw cases for evacuation. Wired asking ADVS 33rd Div re lending him M.V.S personnel or furnishing conducting party if he was using SAULTY Railhead.	

A5834 Wt. W4973/M687 750,000 8/16 D. D. & L. Ltd. Forms/C.2118/13.

Instructions regarding War Diaries and Intelligence Summaries are contained in F. S. Regs., Part II. and the Staff Manual respectively. Title pages will be prepared in manuscript.

WAR DIARY

or

~~INTELLIGENCE SUMMARY.~~

(Erase heading not required.)

Army Form C. 2118.

Place	Date	Hour	Summary of Events and Information	Remarks and references to Appendices
POMMIER	16/4/17		Inspected animals of 17th Manchesters, they were in very good condition	
" "	17/4/17.		Inspected animals of 2nd Yorks (poor condition) & 15th Liverpools (very good). Inspected 19th Manchesters, looking fairly well.	
" "	18/4/17		VO detailed to take over 206 M.G Coy at MONDICOURT & SAULTY, by DDVS reports this unit not at either place, notified D.D.V.S. Inspected animals of 21st Infy Bde HQ (looking well) also 202 Coy RE which were also in good condition. DDVS instructs to take over vety charge of 6th Bn Canadian Railway Troops at GOMBREMETZ, & also inspect the unit for MANGE; CAPT METIVIER detailed. Received vety instruments from Advanced Vety Store, on repayment (£1.9.6) to replace deficiencies in farriers wallets of different units.	
ACHICOURT	19.4.17		Div. HQ moved to ACHICOURT. 40th MVS to change billets from LARBRET to 56th Div MVS at AGNY CHATEAU, to be carried out by 21st inst.	
" "	20.4.17		Visited 56th Div MVS & OC has arranged exchange of billets with 40th MVS. Entraining horses from AGNEZ-les-DUISANS & ARRAS by arrangements with R.T.O's. Took over charge of 30 Div RA (148 & 149 Bdes) 56th Div RA (280 & 281 Bdes) & 293 AFA Bde.	
" "	21.4.17		Notified ADVS 56th Div to take over 6th Bn Canadian Ry Troops at Gombremetz. New allocation of units received, & work allotted to VO's. Inspected 293 AFA Bde. BAC (poor) A & B Btys (fair). A new scheme, the Corps M.V.S detachment started. 40th M.V.S supplies 1 Cpl & 3 OR to report to VII Corps HQ VO at Town Major's BEAUMETZ, 23rd inst 11am. 40th MVS completed its move from LARBRET to AGNY CHATEAU.	

Instructions regarding War Diaries and Intelligence Summaries are contained in F. S. Regs., Part II. and the Staff Manual respectively. Title pages will be prepared in manuscript.

WAR DIARY
or
~~INTELLIGENCE SUMMARY.~~
(Erase heading not required.)

Army Form C. 2118.

Place	Date	Hour	Summary of Events and Information	Remarks and references to Appendices
ACHICOURT	22.4.17		Paid Field Cashier VII Corps £1.9.6 for veterinary instruments, to complete Farriers Wallets in Division	
" "	23.4.17		Forwarded to DDVS Third Army, the percentage of animals unfit for work owing to poor condition & debility, but being kept owing to shortage of remounts. 149 Bde R.F.A. were the highest percentage = 30 poor animals or 5% of present strength.	
" "	24.4.17		Inspected 56th Div DAC. & found animals in fair condition. Saw a suspicious case of Mange in a Gendarme's horse of Div HQ, had it clipped & isolated for observation. Visited M.V.S. & saw animals for evacuation.	
" "	25.4.17		M.V.S. now entraining sick at ARRAS. Went up to Artillery Wagon lines & inspected 149 Bde & 30th DAC, all animals improving & going out to graze daily.	
" "	26.4.17		Inspected ~~...~~ 30th Div Train in evening, on the whole, all looking very well. Visited M.V.S. & saw animals for evacuation.	
" "	27.4.17		V.O's brought Weekly Returns to the office.	
" "	28.4.17		A.DVS. 15th Div arrived, & I handed over charge of 30th Div, 56 Div Artillery & 293 A.F.A. Bde. 15th Div M.V.S. occupied billets of 40th M.V.S. at AGNY CHATEAU.	
" "	29.4.17		Division moved to back area ROELLECOURT (near ST POL).	
ROELLECOURT	30.4.17		40th M.V.S. arrived in new area, & went to ROCOURT ST LAURENT, about 1½ mile from Div HQ. Can entrain sick animals from ST POL. 40th M.V.S. left behind 1 NCO & 6 men with 15th Div M.V.S. to help as conducting parties.	

R.A. Goodwin [?] Major A.V.C.
A.D.V.S. 30th Div.

A5834 Wt. W4973/M687 750,000 8/16 D. D. & L. Ltd. Forms/C.2118/13.

A.A. Goodeve Ch.
Major AVC

A.D.V.S. 30th Div

Secret.

Vol 19

War Diary

-of-

A. D. V. S. 30th Divn

for the Month of

May 1917

Volume 19.

Instructions regarding War Diaries and Intelligence Summaries are contained in F. S. Regs., Part II. and the Staff Manual respectively. Title pages will be prepared in manuscript.

WAR DIARY
or
INTELLIGENCE SUMMARY.
(Erase heading not required.)

Army Form C. 2118.

Volume 19.

Place	Date	Hour	Summary of Events and Information	Remarks and references to Appendices
ROELLECOURT	1.5.17		Visited M.V.S new billet. Good buildings + water for sick animals.	
			Went to see R.T.O. St Pol + arranged for trucks for evacuating sick.	
" "	2.5.17		Inspected animals of Div HQ + A.P.M. all looking well.	
" "	3.5.17		Div HQ moved to Oeuf about 4 miles E of St Pol.	
OEUF	4.5.17		40th M.V.S moved to OEUF.	
			I went on 10 days leave to England. Capt. WILLIAMSON AV.C. OC 40 MVS acting for me.	
" "	14.5.17		Returned from leave.	
WILLEMAN	15.5.17		Divisional HQ moved to WILLEMAN, MVS remains at OEUF (about 2 miles from WILLEMAN).	
			Went to HQ. 150 AFA Bde to give Summary of Evidence re CAPT WOOF AVC overstaying his leave.	
" "	16.5.17		Visited M.V.S + saw two cases of MANGE from 30th Div. Train.	
" "	18.5.17		Inspected animals of Div HQ, all looking well.	
			APM handed a stray Rider in to M.V.S.	
" "	19.5.17		Inspected transport animals of 90th Infy Bde, all looking very well except 2nd R Scots Fusiliers, in which there were about 10 poor animals.	
			Also 201st Coy RE looking well.	
			95th Field Ambulance poor but improving.	
" "	20.5.17		Inspected Sig Coy HQ. looking well.	
PERNES	21.5.17		Division moved to PERNES, also M.V.S.	
NORRENT-FONTES	22.5.17		Div moved to St HILAIRE area (1st Army) Div HQ + M.V.S to NORRENT FONTES.	
			One horse of Div Train too lame to march (Sandcrack) reported left behind with French inhabitant at NUNCQ. Informed DDVS. Third Army.	

A5834 Wt. W4973/M687 750,000 8/16 D. D. & L. Ltd. Forms/C.2118/13.

Instructions regarding War Diaries and Intelligence Summaries are contained in F. S. Regs., Part II. and the Staff Manual respectively. Title pages will be prepared in manuscript.

WAR DIARY
or
~~INTELLIGENCE SUMMARY.~~
(Erase heading not required.)

Army Form C. 2118.

Place	Date	Hour	Summary of Events and Information	Remarks and references to Appendices
NORRENT-FONTES	24.5.17		Div HQ & M.V.S moved to STEENBECQUE (2nd Army Area) Went to HAZEBROUCK & visited DDVS. 2nd Army, & received instruction re Weekly Returns & Evacuation of Sick.	
STEENBECQUE	25.5.17		Div HQ & M.V.S moved to CAESTRE.	
CAESTRE	26.5.17		Division & M.V.S moved to WATOU. Up to present only 2 animals have been left behind since the division started marching.	
WATOU	27.5.17		Went to WINNEZEELE & inspected HQ 21st Infy Bde, 2nd Yorks, 96 Field Ambulance & No 4 Coy Div Train, all animals in good condition especially 96 Fld Ambulance.	
"	28.5.17		Three cases of Mange admitted by M.V.S. 2 from 17th K. Liverpool Regt & 1 from 19th Manchesters. Inspected 19th Mchts, looking well, & improved during last month. Notified by DDVS 2nd Army that a horse left behind at HUNCQ, & since collected was found to be suffering from Sarcoptic Mange at M.V.S.	
"	29.5.17		Inspected 148 Bde R.F.A. after their march, considerable improvement amongst all animals.	
"	30.5.17		Division moved to BRANDHOEK & M.V.S to G 14. b. 4. 4 (Sheet 28) very good billet.	
BRANDHOEK	31.5.17		Inspected 21st M.G Coy. 2nd Wilts. 19th Manchesters. 18th K.L.R. 19th K.L.R. & 2nd BEDS. Two cases Mange in 2nd WILTS, & 2 Mange & Debility in 19 K.L.R. Also inspected 11th S. LANCS, which showed great improvement.	

A.A. Goodall
Major AVC
A.D.V.S. 30th Div.

R.A. Goodenall [?]
Major AVC.
ADVS. 30th Div

Secret.

War Diary

of

D. A. D. V. S. 30th Div.

for the month of

June 1917

Volume XX

Instructions regarding War Diaries and Intelligence Summaries are contained in F. S. Regs., Part II. and the Staff Manual respectively. Title pages will be prepared in manuscript.

WAR DIARY
or
INTELLIGENCE SUMMARY.
(Erase heading not required.)

Army Form C. 2118.

Vol 20

ADVS. 30th Div. Vol XX

Place	Date	Hour	Summary of Events and Information	Remarks and references to Appendices
BRANDHOEK H7c58	1.6.17		Visited M.V.S. & arranged for evacuation as per DDVS 2nd Army orders by road in two stages.	
" "	2.6.17		Inspected 149 Bde RFA. all animals improved especially D "Battery".	
" "	3.6.17		M.V.S evacuated sick by road, only using one stage.	
" "	4.6.17		Inspected 17th & 20th K Liverpools. 6 horses suffering from "Gas shells" 1 died 1 serious, 4 slight.	
" "	5.6.17		Sent weekly inspection report to G.O.C. Inspected No I & II Sections DAC, all looking well.	
" "	6.6.17		Inspected B Echelon DAC. Very good condition. 1 case Sarcoptic Mange. All cases of animals suffering from 'Gas Poisoning' doing well, & have had no treatment.	
" "	7.6.17		Went round lines of 89th Infy Bde.	
" "	8.6.17		Attended M.V.S Advanced Collecting Post at H.16.a.4.9. Went to Poperinghe to try to arrange with Belgian butchers the sale of horses, owing to shortage of customers they can only take one horse per week. Visited X Corps M.V. Detachment where the M.V.S has to send cases for evacuation found it full up & received wire from DDVS Second Army that it had stopped receiving, except for cases unable to go by road to hospital.	
" "	9.6.17		Went 30th DAC & saw animals being treated with Iodoform for Ophthalmia does not appear to be as good a treatment as Zinc Sulph lotion or Argyrol.	
" "	10.6.17		Visited transport of 90th Infy Bde. HQ.	

A5834 Wt. W4973/M687 750,000 8/16 D. D. & L. Ltd. Forms C. 2118/13.

Instructions regarding War Diaries and Intelligence Summaries are contained in F. S. Regs., Part II. and the Staff Manual respectively. Title pages will be prepared in manuscript.

WAR DIARY
or
INTELLIGENCE SUMMARY.
(*Erase heading not required.*)

Army Form C. 2118.

ADVS. 30th Div. Vol XX.

Place	Date	Hour	Summary of Events and Information	Remarks and references to Appendices
BRANDHOEK	11-6-17		Visited 30th DAC & evacuated two horses for Sarcoptic Mange, & also 1 horse from 19th K. Liverpools.	
			Came under Fifth Army	
			Received wire from DDVS Third Army that 149 & 150 Bdes R.FA, were to be tested with Mallein, owing to Glanders being found at BOISLEAUX-au-MONT.	
" "	12.6.17		Visited 84th AFA Bde & evacuated 8 cases Sarcoptic Mange, all from one Sub. Section. 5th RHA Bde, 84th AFA Bde, 113 AFA Bde. came under this division for administration	
" "	13.6.17		232 & 282 AFA Bde joined this division. Visited all AFA VOs.	
			Sent advance Party from MVS to take over MVS billet of 47th Div at G34.b.8.10.	
RENINGHELST	14.6.17		Div HQ moved to RENINGHELST also my office. M.V.S to move on Saturday 16th after evacuating all sick.	
			DDVS & DDR Fifth Army called at my office.	
			Visited 232 AFA Bde.	
			232 & 282 AFA Bdes now attached to 8th Div.	
			Went to 47th M.V.S & found out where their M.V.S. ACP has been located, but as they had not collected any animals there, we did not take it over.	
" "	15.6.17		Under instructions from DDVS, sent non walking cases to X Corps M.V. Detachment	
			V.O's brought in weekly returns.	
			Visited M.V.S in afternoon & saw all cases for evacuation.	
" "	16.6.17		Visited 30th DAC & asked Farriers re Mule shoes being right size or if they required a 15½ size, latter thought necessary. Reported same.	
" "			Transferred Sgt YOUNG AVC from C Bty 148 Bde to HQ 89th Bde.	
	17.6.17		Commenced Mallein Testing 149 Bde. 1 Section from each Bty daily.	
			Distributed Remounts to Units. Saw CRE re shortage of water & had more pumped into reservoirs & troughs.	

A5834 Wt. W4973/M687. 750,000 8/16 D. D. & L. Ltd. Forms/C.2118/13.

Instructions regarding War Diaries and Intelligence Summaries are contained in F. S. Regs., Part II. and the Staff Manual respectively. Title pages will be prepared in manuscript.

WAR DIARY
or
~~INTELLIGENCE SUMMARY.~~
(Erase heading not required.)

Army Form C. 2118.

D.A.D.V.S. 30th Divn. Vol XX

Place	Date	Hour	Summary of Events and Information	Remarks and references to Appendices
~~18.6.~~	18.6.17		Inspected animals tested for Glanders.	
RENINGHELST.			M.V.S handed over 5 Riders from their Establishment to Div Train (QMG 6314 QAOd/23/4/17.	
" "	19.6.17		Inspected animals tested for Glanders.	
			Established M.V.S. a Collecting Post at H26. a. 8 8.	
" "	20.6.17		Attended Conference at St OMER. re ADVS duties with Corps.	
			Inspected lab of Malleined cases. 624 tested all passed.	
" "	21.6.17		Visited 149 Bde R.F.A + 84 A.F.A Bde. Evacuated several Mange cases from each.	
			Also visited 155 AFA Bde.	
" "	22.6.17		V.O's brought weekly returns to office.	
			Received orders to go to 4th Cavalry Division as A.D.V.S.	
" "	23.6.17		Arranged with Staff Captain RA re malleining 148 Bde. R.F.A.	
			Handed over to CAPT WILLIAMSON AVC.	
" "	24.6.17		Arranged with V.O's to visited units.	
" "	25.6.17		Inspected 19th K.L.R. as case of stomatitis found in mange case 23.V.H. no signs of disease furnished report to D.D.V.S.	
	26.6.17		Inspected 2nd R. Scots Fus. sent two suspicious cases (mange) to M.V.S. Inspected B Echelon D.A.C. V. G. condition. Inspected Malleined animals 148th Bde.	

A5834 Wt. W4973/M687 750,000 8/16 D. D. & L. Ltd. Forms/C.2118/13.

Instructions regarding War Diaries and Intelligence Summaries are contained in F. S. Regs., Part II. and the Staff Manual respectively. Title pages will be prepared in manuscript.

WAR DIARY
or
INTELLIGENCE SUMMARY.
(*Erase heading not required.*)

Army Form C. 2118.

D.A.D.V.S. Vol XX. 30th Div.

Place	Date	Hour	Summary of Events and Information	Remarks and references to Appendices
	1917.			
RENINGHELST.	27.6.		Inspected D 148 regarding mange ordered two cases in isolation to M.V.S. animals good condn. Inspected. 16th Manch. 1 mange sent to M.V.S. condn Good. H.Q. 90th Inf Bde Good except for 1 poor mule 18th Manch Very Good 17th Manch Good 1 poor mule.	
	28.6.		D.D.V.S. Fifth Army & A.D.V.S. II Corps called & inspected D148. Inspected malleined animals 148 Bde. also animals of A Batty 148. Fairly Good. B Batty Good D Batty Fairly Good.	
	29.6		V.Os called with Returns. arranged inspections for ensuing week.	
	30.6.		Inspected 149 Bde R.F.A. very wet day Horses under cover, standings very bad, pointed out how might be improved A Batty at work mending them. all Fairly good condition. ordered two animals D149 to M.V.S. (mange)	

D. H. Williamson Major A.V.C.
D.A.D.V.S. 30th Division

Secret.

Vol. 21

War Diary
of
D.A.D.V.S. 30th Div
for the month of
July 1917

Volume 21

Army Form C. 2118.

Instructions regarding War Diaries and Intelligence Summaries are contained in F. S. Regs., Part II. and the Staff Manual respectively. Title pages will be prepared in manuscript.

WAR DIARY
or
INTELLIGENCE SUMMARY.
(Erase heading not required.)

DADVS. 30th Div. vol XXI

Place	Date 1917	Hour	Summary of Events and Information	Remarks and references to Appendices
RENINGHELST.	1-7		at M.V.S.	
	2-7.		Inspected 89th Inf/Bde.	
			Saw A.D.V.S. II Corps at his office.	
	3-7.		Inspected 30 D.A.C. C.148 R.F.A. + Divl Train.	
	4-7.		Inspected 13 A.F.Arty Bde. Visited Horse Bath at POPERINGHE + reported to G.O.C. R.A. re mange.	
	5-7.		Called at A.D.V.S. office arranged with re coy Train re dipping.	
	6-7		Saw A.D.V.S. re dipping visited Advd Post M.V.S.	
	7-7		Moved to NORDAUSQUES.	
NORDAUSQUES	8-7		Office work + arranging for duties of M.V.S. in training area.	
	9-7		Proceeded on leave to U.K. for 10 days.	

A5834 Wt. W4973/M687 750,000 8/16 D. D. & L. Ltd. Forms/C.2118/13.

Army Form C. 2118.

WAR DIARY
or
INTELLIGENCE SUMMARY.
(Erase heading not required.)

Instructions regarding War Diaries and Intelligence Summaries are contained in F. S. Regs., Part II. and the Staff Manual respectively. Title pages will be prepared in manuscript.

D.D.V.S. 30th Div. Vol XXI

Place	Date 1917	Hour	Summary of Events and Information	Remarks and references to Appendices
NORDAUSQUES	9/7		Took over duties D.A.D.V.S, Major Williamson having proceeded on leave 9/7 – 19/7: Inspected animals Hdqts Division, Divisional Signal Coy (R.E.) M.M.P. visited Watten to find out location of No 106 Coy R.E (15th Division), placed under veterinary administration of this Division: unable to trace this unit: inspected the animals of No 4 Coy 30th Divisional Train and 98th Field Ambulance.	
	10/7		Visited No 3 Coy 30th Divisional Train: Proceeded to EPERLECQUES to make arrangements for evacuation of sick animals through 22nd M.V.S of the 11th Division: visited 98th Field Ambulance. Selected 1 Officer and 2 N.C.O's from Infantry Units to attend course of Veterinary instruction at Calais.	
	11/7		Visited Hdqts 21st Infantry Brigade and inspected the animals of each Battalion	
	12/7		Inspected the animals of Hdqts and No 3 Coy 30th Divisional Train: also the animals of 19th Manchester Regiment and 2nd Yorks: Instructed to take over charge of 25th Infantry Brigade at LICQUES:	
	13/7		Inspected the animals of No 4 Coy 8th Divisional Train at GUEMY: also visited Nos 2, 3, & 4 Coys 30th Div Train: 18th Battalion K.L.R, 19th Manchester Regiment and 2nd Yorks: Office, Returns	
	14/7		Inspected 17th and 19th Battalions K.L.R G.O.C's inspection of Brigade Companies of 30th Divisional Train	

A5834 Wt. W4973/M687 750,000 8/16 D. D. & L. Ltd. Forms/C.2118/13.

Instructions regarding War Diaries and Intelligence Summaries are contained in F. S. Regs., Part II. and the Staff Manual respectively. Title pages will be prepared in manuscript.

WAR DIARY
or
INTELLIGENCE SUMMARY.
(Erase heading not required.)

Army Form C. 2118.

8th Div. 30th Div. Vol XXI.

Place	Date	Hour	Summary of Events and Information	Remarks and references to Appendices
	1917			
NORDAUSQUES	15/7		Inspected animals of HdQrs Division, Divisional Signal Coy (R.E.) M.M.P. Office, arrangements for Dipping two Infantry Brigades:	
	16/7		Office, completed dipping arrangements: Inspected the animals of 25th Infantry Brigade, 25th Field Ambulance, and No 4 Coy 8th Divisional Train: proceeded to horse-lines of 2nd York Regiment to see case of Tetanus also HdQrs Divisional Train to see sick horse left behind by No 3 Coy.	
	17/7		Visited 2nd Royal Scot Fusiliers: Office, checking Indents:	
	18/7		Visited 40th Mobile Veterinary Section	
	19/7		Divisional move to STEENVOORDE	
STEENVOORDE	20/7		Inspected 226th M.G. Coy, which joined Division, as a new unit. Major Williamson AVC returned from leave.	
			H.M. McTurner Capt AVC a/D.A.D.V.S.	

A5834 Wt. W4973/M687 750,000 8/16 D. D. & L. Ltd. Forms/C.2118/13.

Instructions regarding War Diaries and Intelligence Summaries are contained in F. S. Regs., Part II. and the Staff Manual respectively. Title pages will be prepared in manuscript.

WAR DIARY
or
INTELLIGENCE SUMMARY.
(Erase heading not required.)

D.D.V.S. 30th Div. Vol XXI

Army Form C. 2118.

Place	Date	Hour	Summary of Events and Information	Remarks and references to Appendices
	1917			
STEENVOORDE	20.7		Took over from Capt Meteric on return from leave.	
	21.7		Attended conference A.D.V.S. II Corps. visited M.V.S. at RENINGHELST.	
	22.7		Inspected H.d.qrs Division M.M.P. & Divisional Cyc Coy.	
	23.7		Inspected 18th [illegible] 17th K.L.R. 90 M.G.C. H.d.qrs 90 I.B.	
	24.7		Moved to RENINGHELST.	
RENINGHELST	25.7		Inspected 148 & 149 Bdes R.F.A. ordered mange cases to M.V.S.	
	26.7		Inspected D.A.C & 226 M.G.C. completed mallein test no reactors	
	27.7		Office. Inspected [illegible] cases M.V.S. saw A.D.V.S. re reduction of estab. & other matters. Village bombed by aeroplane 10.30 p.m. [illegible] wounded in R.G.A. Heavy Batty.	
	28.7		Inspected [illegible] & 11th R.F.A. Bde ordered 3 cases [illegible] to M.V.S.	
	29.7		Inspected M.V.S.	

A5834 Wt. W4973/M687 750,000 8/16 D. D. & L. Ltd. Forms/C.2118/13.

Instructions regarding War Diaries and Intelligence Summaries are contained in F. S. Regs., Part II. and the Staff Manual respectively. Title pages will be prepared in manuscript.

WAR DIARY
or
INTELLIGENCE SUMMARY.
(Erase heading not required.)

DADVS. 30th Div. Vol. XXI

Army Form C. 2118.

Place	Date	Hour	Summary of Events and Information	Remarks and references to Appendices
	1917			
RENINGHELST	30.7		Inspected 200, 201 & 202 Fd Co R.E. Bent stn Transport & advanced Post M.V.S.	
	31.7		Inspected 18th K.L.R. 2nd Yorks. 2nd Wilts. 21st M.G.C. & saw cases at M.V.S.	

J.K. Williamson Major AVC
DADVS 30th Div

A5834 Wt. W4973/M687 750,000 8/16 D. D. & L. Ltd. Forms/C.2118/13.

Vol 22

War Diary
for
month of
August 1917.

D.A.D.V.S.
30th Divn

Vol XXII

Army Form C. 2118.

WAR DIARY
or
INTELLIGENCE SUMMARY.
(*Erase heading not required.*)

Instructions regarding War Diaries and Intelligence Summaries are contained in F. S. Regs., Part II. and the Staff Manual respectively. Title pages will be prepared in manuscript.

DADVS 30th Division Vol. XXII.

Place	Date 1917	Hour	Summary of Events and Information	Remarks and references to Appendices
RENINGHELST.	1-8.		Inspected HdQrs Div. & twice at M.V.S. inspecting animals for evacn.	
	2-8.		Inspected 149 Bde R.F.A.	
	3-8.		V.Os in conference. visited M.V.S. inspected HdQrs.	
	4-8.		Attended conference II nd Corps HdQrs ADVS.	
	5-8		Moved to GODEWARSVELDE	
GODEWARSVELDE	6 8		Inspected all the Infantry, R.E. & 2 Fld Ambs.	
	7-8.		moved to MERRIS.	
MERRIS	8 8		Inspected HdQrs, called on A.D.V.S IX Corps.	
	9-8		Inspected 98th Fd Ambs. & M.V.S.	
	10 8		Inspected XI S. Lancs, 2nd R.S. Fus & DHQ.	
	11-8		Attended Conference A.D.V.S. IX Corps. moved to ST. JANS CAPPEL.	
ST JANS CAPPEL	12-8		Inspected HdQrs.	
	13-8.		M.V.S. & office	
	14-8.		Inspected 98th Fld Amb. 2nd R.S.F. 19th march 16.17.18 march 90 M.G.C.	
	15-8		M.V.S. HdQrs & office.	

A5834 Wt. W4973/M687 750,000 8/16 D. D. & L. Ltd. Forms/C.2118/13.

Army Form C. 2118.

WAR DIARY
or
INTELLIGENCE SUMMARY
(Erase heading not required.)

Instructions regarding War Diaries and Intelligence Summaries are contained in F. S. Regs., Part II. and the Staff Manual respectively. Title Pages will be prepared in manuscript.

D.A.D.V.S. 30th Div. Vol XXII.

Place	Date 1917	Hour	Summary of Events and Information	Remarks and references to Appendices
ST. JANS CAPPEL	16-8.		Inspected 98th Fld Amb. 17th & 18th Manch 96th Fld Amb 226 M.T.C. Case of ulcerative Cellulitis admitted M.V.S. Received by 149 Bde that morning as Remt.	
	17-8.		M.V.S. & Horse Dips. 7 Batteries 2 Fld Amb & 1 Coy Train dipped.	
	18-8.		Inspected all R.F.A. ordered several Debility cases to M.V.S. attended A.D.V.S. Conference.	
	19-8.		Inspected 89th Inf Bde	
	20-8.		Inspected 90th Inf Bde.	
	21-8.		Hdqrs & M.V.S. Lt Little reported from 3. C.H.D. for duty	
	22-8.		Office & M.V.S.	
	23-8.		Moved to DRANOUTRE. accompanied Selection Board for Brood mares. round R.E. & XI Stores.	
DRANOUTRE	24-8		Office & V.O.s conference.	
	25-8		A.D.V.S. Corps Conference arranged for branding of Brood mares.	
	26-8.		Brood mares branded.	
	27-8		Inspected D.A.C.	
	28-8		Inspected 4 Batteries R.F.A.	
	29-8.		Inspected 21st Inf Bde & Hdqrs 90th Bde.	
	30-8		Inf Units Hdqrs & M.V.S.	
	31-8.		V.O.s in conference.	

H. Williamson Major A.V.C.
D.A.D.V.S. 30th Divn.

War Diary

-of-

D.A.D.V.S. 30th Divn.

for the month of

September 1917.

Volume XXIII

Instructions regarding War Diaries and Intelligence Summaries are contained in F. S. Regs., Part II. and the Staff Manual respectively. Title pages will be prepared in manuscript.

WAR DIARY
or
INTELLIGENCE SUMMARY.
(Erase heading not required.)

Army Form C. 2118.

DADVS. 30th Div. Vol. XXIII

Vol 23

Place	Date 1917	Hour	Summary of Events and Information	Remarks and references to Appendices
DRANOUTRE	1.9		attended conference IX Corps visited MVS. inspected animals D 149.	
"	2.9		Inspected no I Coy D. Train.	
	3.9		Inspected D. 148, 21st Inf Bde, 16th & 17th Manch. Regts.	
	4.9		Inspected with ADVS & H.master IX Corps all batteries of 148 Bde R.F.A.	
	5.9		Inspected with V.O. i/c Arty Bdes all batteries of 149 Bde R.F.A. visited IX Corps Horse Dip & saw animals of Div being dipped. had D.R.O. published re branding ^	
	6.9		ADVS & H.master Corps inspected 149 Bde, Inspected Sigs & MVS.	
	7.9		V.O's in conference.	
	8.9		Conference ADVS IX Corps. inspected H.Qrs.	
	9.9		Saw C.R.E. ref site for Clipping Depot, operating MVS in afternoon	
	10.9		ADVS & H.master inspected D. 148 2nd R S Fus. 2nd Bedfs & 20th K.L.R.	
	11.9		Inspected D 148 & evacuated several, 17th KLR. 19th KLR.	
	12.9		Inspected 117 Lab. Co at S. 36. c. 6. 4.	
	13.9.		Inspected 226 M.G.C.	
	14.9		V.O's in conference visited D 148.	

A5834 Wt. W4973/M687 750,000 8/16 D. D. & L. Ltd. Forms/C.2118/13.

Instructions regarding War Diaries and Intelligence Summaries are contained in F. S. Regs., Part II. and the Staff Manual respectively. Title pages will be prepared in manuscript.

WAR DIARY
or
INTELLIGENCE SUMMARY.
(*Erase heading not required.*)

Army Form C. 2118.

D.D.V.S. 30th Divn. Vol XXIII

Place	Date 1917	Hour	Summary of Events and Information	Remarks and references to Appendices
DRANOUTRE	15.9.		Attended conference IX Corps. Inspected 245 Bde R.F.A. 49th Divn.	
	16.9.		Inspected 246 Bde R.F.A. 49th Divn.	
	17.9		" Det I Cav Res PK.	
	18.9		" whole of 90th Inf Bde.	
	19.9.		" whole of 89th Inf Bde.	
	20.9		" whole of 21st Inf Bde, 97th Fd amb & Divl Sig Co.	
	21.9.		" 98th Fd amb Conference V.Os.	
	22.9.		Conference IX Corps Hdqs	
	23.9		Inspected all coys Divl Train.	
	24.9		Submitted report to G.O.C. Divn re condn of animals, good genly. Inspected A. B & C 148. Bde	
	25.9		Arranged with S.S.O. for extra forage for R.S. Fus. 2nd Bedfs 2nd Wilts 20th K.L.R. D 148, C148 & B149.	
	26.9.		Interview with G.O.C. ref report on animals of Divn. Inspected all batteries 149 Bde.	
	27.9.		Inspected 89th Bde. in company with O.C. Train	
	28.9.		" 21st Bde do. Conference V.Os.	
	29.9.		Conference VIII Corps. Lt K. Amiles reptd for duty from 23 Vety Hospl	
	30.9.		Inspected 90th Bde with O.C. Train, ~~[illegible]~~.	

D.K. Williamson Major A.V.C.
D.D.V.S. 30th Divn.

A5834 Wt. W4973/M687 750,000 8/16 D. D. & L. Ltd. Forms/C.2118/13.

War Diary

— of —

D.A.D.V.S. 30th Divn

for the month of

October 1917

Volume 24.

Instructions regarding War Diaries and Intelligence Summaries are contained in F. S. Regs., Part II. and the Staff Manual respectively. Title pages will be prepared in manuscript.

WAR DIARY
or
INTELLIGENCE SUMMARY.
(*Erase heading not required.*)

Army Form C. 2118.

VOLUME XXIV

D. A. D. V. S. 30th Division

Vol 24

Place	Date	Hour	Summary of Events and Information	Remarks and references to Appendices
	1917			
DRANOUTRE	1·X		Capt Chalk proceeded to 23 Vety Hosp for duty.	
	2·X.		15 animals in 'A' 148 Bde reported wounded by Bombs, none serious, Bombs with instantaneous fuze. 70 yds distant.	
	3·X		Reported on unmanageable animal of 226 M.G. Coy.	
	4·X		Office	
	5·X		Capt Metivier proceeded on leave, took over charge M.V.S.	
	6·X		Conference A.D.V.S. Corps.	
	7·X		M.V.S. & office.	
	8·X.		Interviewed C.R.E. ref Clipping Shed	
	9·X.		M.V.S. & office.	
	10·X.		A.D.V.S. Corps visited M.V.S.	
	11·X.		M.V.S. & office	
	12·X.		V.O.s of Division in Conference.	
	13·X.		Conference A.D.V.S. Corps.	
	14·X.		Arranged for class in skinning of animals saw C.R.E. ref Clipping Depot also Q.	
	15·X.		Went with R.E. officer to WESTOUTRE & saw Clipping shed there, not working, many defects visible.	
	16·X.		Arranged with R.E. officer regarding Spray Bath for Clipping Depot.	
	17·X.		Inspected B. C. & D. Batteries 148 Bde all Good.	

A5834 Wt. W4973/M687 750,000 8/16 D. D. & L. Ltd. Forms/C.2118/13.

Instructions regarding War Diaries and Intelligence Summaries are contained in F. S. Regs., Part II. and the Staff Manual respectively. Title pages will be prepared in manuscript.

WAR DIARY
or
INTELLIGENCE SUMMARY.
(Erase heading not required.)

Army Form C. 2118.

D. A. D. V. S. 30th Division Vol XXIV

Place	Date	Hour	Summary of Events and Information	Remarks and references to Appendices
	1917.			
DRANOUTRE	18.X.		Arranged commencement of Clipping next day & sent notifications	
	19.X.		Clipping begun, men absolutely ignorant of it except 3. Clipped 40. V.Os in conference.	
	20.X.		Conference A.D.V.S. Corps. Inspected 98th Fd Amb,	
	21.X.		Clipping Shed 86 animals. Horse branded & handed over to [illegible] by M.M.P. found in possession of a civilian. Issued report on animal	
	22.X.		Inspected B & D 149 & 96th Fd Amb.	
	23.X.		Saw C.R.E. re water supply for Clipping Depot [illegible]	
	24.X.		Inspected thin lines of C 149 & D 148 horses much improved.	
	25.X.		Inspected thin lines A 149 V. Good also the R.S. Fus. much improved	
	26.X.		V.Os Conference. Inspected D.A.C. & V.G. & 20 K.L.R. T.G. advised re teeth of several thin animals.	
	27.X.		Conference A.D.V.S. Corps. Hastened D.A.D.O.S. re spare parts for Clipper heads.	
	28.X.		Clipping Shed & office.	
	29.X.		Clipping Shed going well 108 animals many blades giving out.	
	30.X.		Went round 148 & 149 Bdes with A.D.V.S. Corps.	
	31.X.		Saw C.R.A. re clipping of Arty Horses. permission given by Corps to leave [illegible] Patch. also regarding [illegible] of [illegible] 148 Bde to send Horses for Clipping	

[signature] Williamson Major A.V.C.
D.A.D.V.S. 30th Div.

A5834 Wt. W4973/M687 750,000 8/16 D. D. & L. Ltd. Forms/C.2118/13.

Secret.

War Diary

of

D.A.D.V.S. 30th Div

for the month of

November 1917

Volume XXV

Instructions regarding War Diaries and Intelligence Summaries are contained in F. S. Regs., Part II. and the Staff Manual respectively. Title pages will be prepared in manuscript.

WAR DIARY
or
~~INTELLIGENCE SUMMARY.~~
(Erase heading not required.)

Army Form C. 2118.

Vol 25

DADVS 30th Divn Vol XXV

Place	Date 1917	Hour	Summary of Events and Information	Remarks and references to Appendices
DRANOUTRE	1.XI		Interviewed D.A.D.O.S. ref Heads for Clipping machines & induced him to wire Base & hasten as present are almost worn out	
			Arranged for inspection of last lot of Remounts issued other units, by A.D.V.S. Corps, I had reported these as being very inferior.	
	2.XI		Accompanied A.D.V.S. Corps during his inspection of Remounts. V.Os in conference	
			Reported A.D.V.S. Corps regarding progress of Clipping	
			Reported to Q. & A.D.V.S. Corps regarding the poor quality of Clipping machines issued, also the difficulty in obtaining spare heads & plates & advising that Clipping would soon have to stop if same not forthcoming.	
	3.XI.		Wrote D.A.D.O.S. ref clipping machines, had D.R.O. published regarding protection of Horse lines from Aircraft Bombs. A.D.V.S. Conference, suggested C.R.O. re dipping of Horses after Clipping.	
	4.XI.		Wrote Camp Comdt ref non-dipping of some of H.d.qrs Horses. issued orders to O.C. M.V.S. regarding issue of Rum to men.	
	5.XI		Proceeded on leave, handed over to Capt McTiernan AVC	

Instructions regarding War Diaries and Intelligence Summaries are contained in F. S. Regs., Part II. and the Staff Manual respectively. Title pages will be prepared in manuscript.

WAR DIARY
or
~~INTELLIGENCE SUMMARY~~.
(Erase heading not required.)

Army Form C. 2118.

D.A.D.V.S 30th Div. Vol XXV

Place	Date	Hour	Summary of Events and Information	Remarks and references to Appendices
Dranoutre	Nov 5th		Took over duties of D.A.D.V.S	
	Nov 6th		Visited clipping Depot and 40th M.V.S: arranged detail of clipping of clipped animals.	
	Nov 7th		Visited 30th Divisional Train: visited Clipping Depot.	
	Nov 8th		Visited 89th Infantry Brigade: arranged detail for clipping animals:	
	Nov 9th		Conference of V.O's and A.V.C.O's: visited clipping Depot: Inspected animals of 90th Infantry Brigade.	
	Nov 10th		Attended Corps Conference with Returns:	
	Nov 11th		Visited Steenvoorde area to arrange for move of M.V.S	
	Nov 12th		Inspected 40th M.V.S: visited clipping Depot	
	Nov 13th		Visited Steenvoorde area to arrange accomodation for Divisional clipping Depot	
	Nov 14th		Visited clipping Depot and 40th M.V.S	
	Nov 15th		Handed over to D.A.D.V.S (5th Australian Division) Clipping Depot: move of Division.	

A5834 Wt. W4973/M687 750,000 8/16 D. D. & L. Ltd. Forms/C.2118/13.

Instructions regarding War Diaries and Intelligence Summaries are contained in F. S. Regs., Part II. and the Staff Manual respectively. Title pages will be prepared in manuscript.

WAR DIARY
or
~~INTELLIGENCE SUMMARY.~~
(Erase heading not required.)

Army Form C. 2118.

D.A.D.V.S. 30th Divn Vol XXV

Place	Date	Hour	Summary of Events and Information	Remarks and references to Appendices
Steenvoorde	Nov 16th		Conference of V.O's and A.V.O's: arranged detail for clipping of animals in new area.	
	Nov 17th		Attended Corps Conference with Returns.	
	Nov 18th		Visited Clipping Depot and 40th M.V.S.	
	Nov 19th		Inspected Nos 2, 3 and 4 Companies 30th Divisional Train:	
	Nov 20th		Inspected Transport Lines of 21st, 89th and 90th Brigade Hdqts: Visited Clipping Depot	
	Nov 21st		Handed over to D.A.D.V.S on his return from leave:	

H.V. Metivier
Capt A.V.C
21/11/17

A5834 Wt. W4973/M687 750,000 8/16 D. D. & L. Ltd. Forms/C.2118/13.

Instructions regarding War Diaries and Intelligence Summaries are contained in F. S. Regs., Part II. and the Staff Manual respectively. Title pages will be prepared in manuscript.

WAR DIARY
or
INTELLIGENCE SUMMARY.
(Erase heading not required.)

Army Form C. 2118.

D.A.D.V.S. 30th Division Vol XXV

Place	Date 1917	Hour	Summary of Events and Information	Remarks and references to Appendices
STEENVOORDE	22.XI		Office work.	
	23.XI		Inspected M.V.S. & Clipping Depot. Conference with V.O.s	
"	24.XI		Inspected HdQrs Division & Divl Sig Coy. Arranged for collection of wounded mules at VLAMERTINGHE. Attended conference VIII Corps	
"	25.XI		Saw Staff Capt 21st Bde ref course of Farriery. P.M. Exam of dog suspected of rabies, no P.M. symptoms.	
	26.XI		Arranged for move of M.V.S. & Clipping Depot to new area. Visited new area & saw camp proposed for M.V.S. reported unfavourably.	
	27.XI		Moved to WESTOUTRE.	
WESTOUTRE	28.XI		Arranged move of M.V.S. & Clipping Depot to ARAGON CAMP tomorrow	
	29.XI		Inspected all batteries of 149 Bde R.F.A. all Good except D which has fallen off slightly. Arranged for clipping to recommence next day.	
	30.XI		Inspected M.V.S. & Clipping Depot also all batteries 148 Bde R.F.A. all Good. V.O's conference	

D.L. Williamson Major A.V.C.
D.A.D.V.S. 30th Division

A5834 Wt. W4973/M687 750,000 8/16 D. D. & L. Ltd. Forms/C.2118/13.

Vol 26

War Diary

-of-

D.A.D.V.S. 30th Divn

for the month

of

December 1917

Volume XXVI.

Army Form C. 2118.

Instructions regarding War Diaries and Intelligence Summaries are contained in F. S. Regs., Part II. and the Staff Manual respectively. Title pages will be prepared in manuscript.

WAR DIARY
or
INTELLIGENCE SUMMARY.
(*Erase heading not required.*)

DADVS 30th Div Vol XXVI

Place	Date	Hour	Summary of Events and Information	Remarks and references to Appendices
	1917			
WESTOUTRE	1 · xii		Conference A.D.V.S. IX Corps.	
			Inspected 89th InfBde, 18th KLR. HdQrs 90th InfBde & 21st MGC	
	2 · xii		Inspected 226 MG Coy DAC & 2nd Yorks & 21st InfBde HdQrs.	
			Saw T.O. 2nd Wilts ref complaint as to state of roads & tracks used by Pack Train	
	3 · xii		Inspected MVS & Clipping Depot.	
			" 90th InfBde & XI Stores.	
			Rearranged Dipping programme.	
	4 · xii		Visited MVS with ADVS Corps to see cases of Ophthalmia	
			Inspected Field Coys RE & 97th Fld Amb.	
	5 · xii		Inspected Divl Sig Coy 98th Fd Amb & HdQrs Div. MVS & Clipping Depot.	
	6 · xii		Accompanied AA & QMG on his inspection of M.V.S. & Clipping Depot.	
			Inspected 96th Fd Amb & horses of 97th on detachment.	
			Forwarded report on bad state of pack roads & tracks.	
			Arranged for opening of Divl Animal Rest Farm.	
	7 · xii		VOs of Div in Conference.	
			Inspected Ophthalmia cases at M.V.S.	
			Inspected all Coys Divisional Train	
			" 2nd Wilts & 19th Manch.	
	8 · xii		ADVS Conference M.V.S. & Clipping Depot arranged for closing of latter	

Instructions regarding War Diaries and Intelligence Summaries are contained in F. S. Regs., Part II. and the Staff Manual respectively. Title pages will be prepared in manuscript.

WAR DIARY
or
INTELLIGENCE SUMMARY.
(Erase heading not required.)

Army Form C. 2118.

DADVS 30th Div Vol XXVI

Place	Date 1917	Hour	Summary of Events and Information	Remarks and references to Appendices
WESTOUTRE	9 XII		MVS & office. Inspected D.149. MVS. HdQrs RA.	
	10 XII		Animal Rest Farm opened, reported to G.O.C. & A.D.V.S. Corps on condn of animals of Div.	
	11 XII		MVS & Rest Farm arranged for hiring of field for Rest Farm.	
	12 XII		Forwarded list of NCOs & 1 offr for Vety Course, Saw S.S.O. ref Bran & extra forage.	
	13 XII		MVS Rest Farm & office.	
	14 XII		V.O's of Division in conference.	
	15 XII		Conference of A.D.V.S. IX Corps Inspected 6th Res Park.	
	16 XII		Arranged for issue of Chaffcutters to Units not in possession. Arranged Vety charge of 11th D.L.I. & 6th K.S.L.I.	
	17 XII		Inspected MVS Rest Farm D.149. A.149 & HdQrs 149 Bde RFA.	
	18 XII		Inspected Evacuation cases at M.V.S.	
	19 XII		Inspected B & C 149 Bde R.F.A. HdQrs 89th Inf Bde.	
	20 XII		Inspected R.E. HdQrs & 98th [illegible]	
	21st XII		V.O's in conference. Inspected HdQrs Div HdQrs RA & M.M.P. Wrote A.P.M. ref waste of oats	
	22 XII		Conference A.D.V.S. IX Corps, inspected proposed sites for M.V.S. reported unsuitable.	
	23 XII		MVS & Rest Farm	
	24 XII		Inspected 2nd Wilts 19th Manch 21 MG Coy 89th MG Coy 17th KLR 2nd Bedf. 19th KLR 20th KLR, HdQrs 21st Inf Bde.	
	25 XII		Office & sports at MVS in afternoon, inspected mens dinners & cookhouse &c.	

A5834 Wt. W4973/M687 750,000 8/16 D. D. & L. Ltd. Forms/C.2118/13.

Instructions regarding War Diaries and Intelligence Summaries are contained in F. S. Regs., Part II. and the Staff Manual respectively. Title pages will be prepared in manuscript.

WAR DIARY
or
INTELLIGENCE SUMMARY.
(*Erase heading not required.*)

Army Form C. 2118.

DADVS 30th Div vol XXVI

Place	Date 1917	Hour	Summary of Events and Information	Remarks and references to Appendices
WESTOUTRE	26.xii		Inspected M.V.S. Kest Farm.	
	27.xii		Saw Staff Captain 89th Inf Bde ref A.V.C. Sergeant & 28th M.V.S. ref horse of 96th Fd Amb.	
	28.xii		V.O's in conference.	
	29.xii		ill	
	30.xii		D.V.S. Fourth Army & A.D.V.S. IX Corps inspected M.V.S. Kest Farm.	
	31.xii		Saw animals at M.V.S. for evacuation.	
			Inspected horse of M. VERBORCH refugee in company with Lt Col Perich Belgian Vety Service in reference to claim for damage sustained in March last.	
			D.R. Wilkinson Major A.V.C.	
			DADVS 30th Div	

A5834 Wt. W4973/M687 750,000 8/16 D. D. & L. Ltd. Forms/C.2118/13.

DAD✓S

Secret.

War Diary

of

D.A.D.V.S. 30th Div

for the month of

January 1918

Vol. XXVII

XXVII

Army Form C. 2118.

Instructions regarding War Diaries and Intelligence Summaries are contained in F. S. Regs., Part II. and the Staff Manual respectively. Title pages will be prepared in manuscript.

WAR DIARY
or
INTELLIGENCE SUMMARY.

(Erase heading not required.)

DADVS 30th Div Vol XXVII

VR 27

Place	Date 1918	Hour	Summary of Events and Information	Remarks and references to Appendices
WESTOUTRE	1. I		Inspected Hdqrs Div Hdqrs RA MMP. A 148 & C 148 Bde RFA	
	2. I		Inspected 90th Inf Bde, B & D Batts 148 Bde RFA. 97th Fd Amb. MVS	
	3. I		Inspected XI Lancs. 200 201 & 202 Fd Coys RE. Advd Transport lines. Saw CRE. re poor cond of some of 201 Coys mules & pointed out neglect & use chaffcutter.	
	4. I		Inspected Divl Train. 226 M.G. Coy. V.Os in conference. Forwarded Report to G.O.C re cond of animals in Division.	
	5. I		MVS office	
	6. I		Moved to BLARINGHEM.	
BLARINGHEM.	7. I		Arrangements re move to BOVES area	
	8. I		Inspected No 3 Coy Divl Train.	
	9. I		Moved to CORBIE. Snowstorm	
CORBIE	10. I		Office arrived in evg being held up previous night in snow near DOULLENS.	
	11. I		Inspected 2nd K.S. Lan. re mange & 90th Bde Hdqrs.	
	12. I		Called on D.D.V.S. re evacuation & collections & conducting party. Forwarded memo to Q re disinfection of French Stalls.	
	13. I		Arranged with A.G. MVS & O.O. Army Tps re evacuation of animals left by other Divns	
	14. I		Moved to NESLE. Inspected possible billets for MVS at BILLANCOURT. reported to Q unfavourably.	
NESLE.	15. I		Found billet for MVS at NESLE. Inspected mange infected places & directed their being placed out of bounds &c.	

A5834 Wt. W4973/M687 750,000 8/16 D. D. & L. Ltd. Forms/C.2118/13.

Instructions regarding War Diaries and Intelligence Summaries are contained in F. S. Regs., Part II. and the Staff Manual respectively. Title pages will be prepared in manuscript.

WAR DIARY
or
INTELLIGENCE SUMMARY.
(*Erase heading not required.*)

Army Form C. 2118.

D.A.D.V.S. 30th Division Vol XXVII

Place	Date 1918.	Hour	Summary of Events and Information	Remarks and references to Appendices
AESLE	16.7		Inspected 98th Fd Amb & Civilian horse at MESNIL with mange reported to Q.	
-	17.7		M.V.S. Sig Coy & Hdqrs inspected.	
	18.7		V.O's in Conference.	
	19.7		Moved to ERCHEU.	
ERCHEU	20.7		Inspected Horse billets regarding disinfection necessary arranged for Rest Farm at SUCRERIE, Case of mange LIBERMONT	reported to Q.
	21.7		Inspected 89th Inf Bde & 149 Bde R.F.A. with A.D.V.S. Corps.	
	22.7		Inspected animals at M.V.S. for evacuation 2nd R.S. Fus.	
	23.7		Inspected 148 Bde & 2 Sections D.A.C.	
	24.7		Inspected 17th French Regt 3 Coy Train & 98th Fd Amb.	
	25.7		Inspected No 1 Sect D.A.C & No 1 Coy Train	
	26.7		Went to new area & saw A.D.V.S. French Division, who stated that mange had occurred at GUIVENCOURT & OGNES. unable to furnish any details regarding places or number affected. Saw V.O. 10th Dragoons, no contagious disease.	
	27.7		Inspected 97th Fd Amb.	
	28.7		Moved to CHAUNY	
CHAUNY.	29.7		Inspected Nos 3 & 4 Coys Train & M.V.S. saw V.O. of French Army at OGNES. stated no mange lately & all places disinfected	
	30.7		Inspected 89th Bde Hdqrs.	
	31.7		Inspected 2nd Yorks 2nd Wilts 18th Liverpools & 21st M.G. Coy	

D.K. Williamson Major A.V.C.
D.A.D.V.S. 30th Divn

A5834 Wt. W4973/M687 750,000 8/16 D. D. & L. Ltd. Forms/C.2118/13.

War Diary

-of-

D.A.D.V.S. 30th Divn

for the Month

-of-

February 1918.

Volume XXVIII.

14

Instructions regarding War Diaries and Intelligence Summaries are contained in F. S. Regs., Part II. and the Staff Manual respectively. Title pages will be prepared in manuscript.

WAR DIARY
or
INTELLIGENCE SUMMARY.
(Erase heading not required.)

Army Form C. 2118.

DADVS 30th Div Vol XXVIII

Vol 28

Place	Date 1918	Hour	Summary of Events and Information	Remarks and references to Appendices
CHAUNY.	1. II		Office ~~moved to V~~	
	2. II		moved to VILLEQUIER-AUMONT. saw 58th Div ref moves & locations.	
VILLEQUIER-AUMONT.	3. II		Inspected 19th Manchesters.	
	4. II		Inspected animals at M.V.S. for evacuation. ADVS conference.	
	5. II		Inspected 385 Forestry Coy RE. & 4 Section 21st Res Park.	
	6. II		Inspected 151st Labour Coy.	
	7. II		Inspected 503rd Field Coy RE. several mange to MVS. 19th KL Regt.	
	8. II		" 17th KL Regt & 89th Bde Hdqrs. Saw OC MVS ref move.	
	9. II		Divl Hdqrs ERCHEU.	
ERCHEU.	10. II		Took over billets for MVS & Rest Farm, which arrived today. Saw SSO. ref extra forage.	
	11. II		Inspected MVS & Rest Farm, arranged for use of field at Quesnoy for animals in Rest Farm.	
	12. II		Inspected (in XVIII Corps Area) 200 Fd Co RE. not looking so well. 201st Fd Co much Impd sent one animal to Rest Farm	
	13. II		Inspected 202nd Fd Coy RE. V.G. sent one to Rest Farm. 2nd Bedfords. 1 to Rest Farm.	
	14. II		Inspected 2nd RS Fusiliers. picking up again, one for Rest Farm when Remounts arrive	
	15. II		Inspected A.B.C & D Batteries 148 Bde all Good 2 from D & 2 from B for Rest Farm. 2 & 3 Sects DAC. V.G.	
	16. II		MVS & Rest Farm. MVS completed repairs & setting up of Horse power Chaffcutter for use of Infy Bdes, arranged with Q as to its use by them.	
	17. II		Divl Hdqrs & Divnl Arty. Saw SSO ref extras for Rest Farm. states very difficult to obtain.	
	18. II		Inspected A.149. still V.G. but not looking so well. B looking rather better 4 to Rest Farm. C. V.G. saw incontacts & one fresh case of mange very slight. D Batty V.G. 2 to Rest Farm	

A5834 Wt. W4973/M687 750,000 8/16 D. D. & L. Ltd. Forms/C.2118/13.

WAR DIARY
or
INTELLIGENCE SUMMARY.
(Erase heading not required.)

Instructions regarding War Diaries and Intelligence Summaries are contained in F. S. Regs., Part II. and the Staff Manual respectively. Title pages will be prepared in manuscript.

Army Form C. 2118.

D.A.D.V.S. 30th Divn Vol XXVIII

Place	Date 1918.	Hour	Summary of Events and Information	Remarks and references to Appendices
ERCHEU.	19. 11		Inspected 16th Manchesters & 97th Field Amb. sent one animal to M.V.S. for debility & old age.	
	20. 11		Proceeded to forward area to reconnoitre site for M.V.S. saw 90th Bde en route transport looking very well	
			Saw A.D.V.S. Corps ref FERME ANGLAISE as site for M.V.S. very suitable sent advance party to take possn.	
	21. 11		Inspected animals at M.V.S. for evacuation, also animals at Rest Farm directed 14 to be returned	
			to duty, [illegible] except one horse of 'A' 148	
			Held [illegible] conference [illegible] duties in new area, issued copies of detail to [illegible] units.	
	22. 11		Took over duties of D.A.D.V.S during absence of Major D.R. Williamson AVC on Leave	
HAM	23 11		Divisional Move: Divisional H.d.qts at Ham: attended conference A.D.V.S XVIII Corps.	
	24 11		A.D.V.S XVIII Corps visited Section: M.V.S to run XVIII Corps V.C.C.S.	
	25 11		Inspected Remounts at HAM Railhead: visited 97th Field Ambulance	
Ourg	26 11		Division moved to Ourg:	
	27 11		Arranged cold Shoeing course, visited M.V.S and Rest Farm.	
	28 11		Visited Nos 2 Coy 30th Div. Train and 96 Field Ambulance: Office	

H.B. McEttrick Capt
A/DADVS
30th Division.

War Diary

-of-

D.A.D.V.S. 30th Divn.

for the month of

March 1915

Volume XXIX.

24

Instructions regarding War Diaries and Intelligence Summaries are contained in F. S. Regs., Part II. and the Staff Manual respectively. Title pages will be prepared in manuscript.

WAR DIARY
or
INTELLIGENCE SUMMARY.
(Erase heading not required.)

Army Form C. 2118.

Vol 29

D.A.D.V.S Vol. XXIX

30th Division.

Place	Date 1918	Hour	Summary of Events and Information	Remarks and references to Appendices
Bury	1 III		Office: V.O's Conference and Returns	
	2 III		Conference A.D.V.S Corps: visited Divisional Rest Farm with A.D.V.S Corps.	
	3 III		Office: Veterinary Service arrangements for Active Operations: V.O's Conference resume.	
	4 III		Veterinary attendance arranged for attached Labour Corps: visited Nos 2+4 Coys 30th Divisional Train.	
	5 III		Attended HAM Railhead re entrainment of sick animals to Vety Hospital	
	6 III		Inspected C/149 Brigade R.F.A: animals good.	
	7 III		At M.V.S and Divisional Rest Farm.	
	8 III		Office: V.O's Conference and Returns.	
	9 III		At Divisional Rest Farm: arrangements made for starting a Sulphur Gas Chamber.	
	10 III		A.D.V.S Corps visited M.V.S: Major Williamson D.A.D.V.S returned from leave.	

H. H. Martin Capt A.V.C

A5834 Wt. W4973/M687 750,000 8/16 D. D. & L. Ltd. Forms/C.2118/13.

Instructions regarding War Diaries and Intelligence Summaries are contained in F. S. Regs., Part II. and the Staff Manual respectively. Title pages will be prepared in manuscript.

WAR DIARY
or
INTELLIGENCE SUMMARY.
(*Erase heading not required.*)

Army Form C. 2118.

D.A.D.V.S. 30th Divn. XXIX

Place	Date 1918	Hour	Summary of Events and Information	Remarks and references to Appendices
DURY	11. iii		Inspected Divl Hdqrs. M.M.P. & Div. Sig Coy.	
	12. iii		Inspected 148 Bde R.F.A. & S.A.A. Section. Received notice of inspection by D.V.S.	
	13. iii		D.V.S. unable to inspect. Conference at A.D.V.S. office, & visited M.V.S. consulted with D.A.D.V.S. 61st Divn ref Sulphur chamber.	
	14. iii		Inspected 16th Manchesters & No 3 Coy Train.	
	15. iii		V.O's conference. inspected 149 Bde R.F.A. forwarded Report on Animals to 30 Div	
	16. iii		Office & M.V.S. Inspected 2nd R. Scots. Fus.	
	17. iii		Inspected machine Gun Batt. 98th Fd amb 17th K.L.R. 18th K.L.R. 19th K.L.R. XI Lancs 20th K.L.R. 2nd Wilts. 2nd Yorks.	
	18. iii		Inspected 200th & 201st R.E. 2nd Bedfords. 97th Field Amb.	
	19. iii		Closed down Animal Rest Farm. Inspected M.V.S. & turn out horses & men	
	20. iii		Inspected 19th Manchesters & 17th Manchester	
	21. iii		Heavy bombardment opened 4.40 am. misty day. 12 casualties reported in R.S.Fus by 11 am. & several around D.H.Q. which was shelled persistently from 6 am. till 9.40 am. 12 pm. moved with rear Echelon KERCHEU arriving 2.30 am. Capt Andrews Capt Little & Lt Miles reported during evening.	

A5834 Wt. W4973 M687 750,000 8/16 D. D. & L. Ltd. Forms/C.2118/13.

Instructions regarding War Diaries and Intelligence Summaries are contained in F. S. Regs., Part II. and the Staff Manual respectively. Title pages will be prepared in manuscript.

WAR DIARY
or
INTELLIGENCE SUMMARY.
(Erase heading not required.)

Army Form C. 2118.

D.D.V.S. 30th Div. Vol. XXIX

Place	Date 1918.	Hour	Summary of Events and Information	Remarks and references to Appendices
ERCHEU.	22. iii	2.30am	arrived. Returns forwarded same day to A.D.V.S. Corps. News received at 12 noon that enemy patrols seen in DURY. went to HAM by car to get M.V.S. moved. (not possible to wire) met M.O.S. en route with 80 sick & wounded from all Divisions of Corps, no trucks available at HAM for evacuation as all taken up with refugees. HAM being heavily shelled whilst there.	
	23. iii	11 a.m.	moved to ROIGLISE. M.V.S. to ROYE. Roads very congested with civilian traffic. helped form stragglers post at SOLENTE collected 700 men & N.C.O.s & several Lewis Guns & returned them under an officer to Divl Hdqrs.	
ROIGLISE.	24. iii		Visited wagon lines Arty near ERCHEU. heard that enemy had taken possession of ESMERY-HALLON & arty retiring on ERCHEU, no enemy to be seen from there. Capt Corbes reported several animals missing. went to M.V.S. & evacuation arranged for evacuation of sick animals that evg saw them put on train. Surplus Supply Transport being sent to ABBEVILLE.	
	25. iii		moved to HANGEST-EN-SANTERRE arrived 6 pm. no billets no billeting officer who had gone to LE PLESSIER by error. left M.O.S. with Arty under French Corps.	
	26. iii	9 a.m.	O.C. M.V.S. arrived to report that he had left ROYE as enemy were shelling & machine gunning that place. an orderly had been sent to Arty with orders to bring back news of a retirement but he had not got through when M.V.S. moved.	

A5834 Wt. W4973/M687 750,000 8/16 D. D. & L. Ltd. Forms/C.2118/13.

Instructions regarding War Diaries and Intelligence Summaries are contained in F. S. Regs., Part II. and the Staff Manual respectively. Title pages will be prepared in manuscript.

WAR DIARY
or
INTELLIGENCE SUMMARY.
(Erase heading not required.)

Army Form C. 2118.

D.A.D.V.S. 30th Div Vol XXIX

Place	Date	Hour	Summary of Events and Information	Remarks and references to Appendices
HANGEST EN SANTERRE	26. iii		O.C. M.V.S. rejoined section at ERCHES & all sick with it. endeavoured to get information as to situation from H.Qrs but failed. directed O.C. M.V.S. to move back to LA NEUVILLE with Infy Transport of Div.	
		1.30 pm	left for BRACHES.	
		2.30 am	arrived BRACHES.	
BRACHES.			Received orders immediately on arrival to move to AILLY. SUR NOYE. directed M.V.S. to Move 6.30 pm.	
AILLY SUR NOYE.		8. pm.	arrived looked for billets for M.V.S. everything in a hopeless muddle, French troops in possession of all available accomodation. M.V.S spent night in a lane.	
	27. iii		Still at AILLY.	
	28. iii		Moved to FOURNCAMPS. for a midday meal & then back to ESTREES arrived 6 pm. found billets for M.V.S. none available for officers. O.C. M.V.S & myself occupied clay floor of a farmhouse full of refugees who chattered the whole night.	
ESTREES. SUR NOYE.	29. iii		Still at ESTREES. visited Infy Transport at ROUVREL	
	30. iii		Entrained at SALEUX in horse truck 5 pm. arrived ST. VALERY SUR. SOMME. 12 midnight, no billets arranged, spent night in cattle truck with 3 other officers. M.V.S coming by road	
ST VALERY SUR. SOMME.	31. iii		Arranged for accommodation for M.V.S. (good & plentiful)	

D. R. Williamson Major AVC
D.A.D.V.S. 30th Div

Secret.

War Diary

for the Month of

April 1918

of

D.A.D.V.S. 30th Division

Volume XXX

27

Instructions regarding War Diaries and Intelligence Summaries are contained in F. S. Regs., Part II. and the Staff Manual respectively. Title pages will be prepared in manuscript.

WAR DIARY
or
INTELLIGENCE SUMMARY.
(Erase heading not required.)

Army Form C. 2118.

DDVS [illegible] 30th Div Vol XXX

Vol 30

Place	Date 1918	Hour	Summary of Events and Information	Remarks and references to Appendices
ST. VALERY Sur SOMME	1-4		Inspected 2, 3 & 4 Coys Divl Train	
	2.4		Inspected 96 & 98th Field Ambs	
	3.4		Inspected M.V.S. & animals for evacuation	
	4.4		Part of Division moved off for entrainment, arranged with D.A.Q.M.G. re [illegible] etc.	
do	5.4	4.40am	Left St Valery	
	5.4.	8 pm	Arrived PROVEN	
PROVEN.	6.4		Called at II Corps with Returns.	
	7.4		Saw A.D.V.S. II Corps & Inspected M.V.S. at new billet on Switch Road	
	7.4		Moved to CANAL BANK Dugouts relieved 1st Division	
CANAL BANK. YPRES	9.4		Inspected 89th Inf Bde. Horses looking very well mules good.	
	10.4		Inspected 14 A. & S. Highlanders on arrival in Division fairly good. Unit Chest in very bad condition. Noted for indent. Inspected 4 Labour Coys & arranged VETY attendance for 18 others. Shelled from 11 pm. till 3 30 am.	
	11.4		Moved to ELVERDINGHE	
ELVERDINGHE	12.4		Returned, saw A.D.V.S. II Corps in afternoon, about move to HERZEELE. 14 D.R. reported [illegible] probably those who should have reported to M.V.S. when acting as V.E.S. at HAM. 2 weeks ago	
	13.4		Moved to ST. SIXTE.	

A5834 Wt. W4973 M687 750,000 8/16 D. D. & L. Ltd. Forms/C.2118/13.

Instructions regarding War Diaries and Intelligence Summaries are contained in F. S. Regs., Part II. and the Staff Manual respectively. Title pages will be prepared in manuscript.

WAR DIARY
or
INTELLIGENCE SUMMARY.
(Erase heading not required.)

Army Form C. 2118.

D.A.D.V.S. 30th Division Vol XXX

Place	Date 1918	Hour	Summary of Events and Information	Remarks and references to Appendices
ST SIXTE	14.4		Orders from A.D.V.S. II Corps to send 14 O.R. from Base to II Corps V.E.S. Inspected probable site for M.V.S.	
	15.4		Inspected 90th Inf/Bde Good.	
	16.4		Inspected 21st Inf/Bde Good & Divnl Sig Co V. Good	
	17.4		Office. unable to carry out inspections owing to attack of lumbago.	
	18.4		do.	
	19.4		do. 90th Bde Transport 3 Coy Train & 96th F.A. [illegible] move tomorrow LEDERZEELE. M.V.S. also [illegible] M.V.S. in [illegible]	
	20.4		moved to CATTERICK. CAMP. G.H.Q. Site near BRANDHOEK Reported A.D.V.S. II Corps that most of Labour Coys had moved & could not be found.	
CATTERICK CAMP	21.4		O.C. i/c Arty Bdes reported shortage of horse shoes & remounts.	
	22.4		Inspection of M.G. Bn. Reported to Q unfavourably on Transport officer, several animals unshod. Shoes had been thrown away & no reserve, also 20 mules shoulder galled, [illegible] in Division	
	23.4		[illegible] instructions to O.C. M.V.S. to detach party for duty with Arty, owing to difficulties in evacuation especially when fighting with French [illegible] of touch with British M.V.S.	
	24.4		Inspected Field Coy R.E. fairly good, one or two thin mules. Camp shelled all day.	
	25.4		[illegible] LEDERZEELE	
	26.4		Inspected M.V.S. & Returned Office. Inspected surplus transport 6th 37th & 49th Division	

A5834 Wt. W4973/M687 750,000 8/16 D. D. & L. Ltd. Forms/C.2118/13.

Army Form C. 2118.

Instructions regarding War Diaries and Intelligence Summaries are contained in F. S. Regs., Part II. and the Staff Manual respectively. Title pages will be prepared in manuscript.

WAR DIARY
or
INTELLIGENCE SUMMARY.
(Erase heading not required.)

D.D.V.S. 30th Divn Vol XXX

Place	Date 1918.	Hour	Summary of Events and Information	Remarks and references to Appendices
BROXEELE	27.4		A.D.V.S. XXII Corps Conference. arranged Vety attendance for units detached	
	28.4		Inspected 96th Field Amb & No 3 Coy Train. V. Good	
	29.4		Arranged Vety attendance 2nd Pontoon Park.	
	30.4		Inspected 97th & 98th Field Ambs. V. Good	

J K Wilkinson Major
D.D.V.S. 30th Div

A5834 Wt. W4973/M687 750,000 8/16 D. D. & L. Ltd. Forms/C.2118/13.

S E C R E T.

W A R D I A R Y.

of.

D.A.D.V.S. 30th. D.I.V.I.S.I.O.N.

for the Month of.

M A Y 1918.

VOLUME. XXXI.

18

Instructions regarding War Diaries and Intelligence Summaries are contained in F. S. Regs., Part II. and the Staff Manual respectively. Title pages will be prepared in manuscript.

DADVS Army Form C. 2118.

WAR DIARY
or
INTELLIGENCE SUMMARY.
(Erase heading not required.)

DADVS 30th Divn Vol XXXI

Vol 31

Place	Date 1918.	Hour	Summary of Events and Information	Remarks and references to Appendices
BRONEELE	1.5.		Inspected MVS Divl Sig Co. & MMP.	
	2.5		Saw sick animals 74th (Yeo) Division	
	3.5		Inspected surplus animals 2nd Army Entrenching Battn for transfer to Remount Section	
	4.5.		Attended Conference ADVS XXII Corps.	
	5.5.		Visited MVS & 90th Bde Hdqrs.	
	6.5.		Visited 23 Vety Hospital & Army Remount Section ref riders	
	7.5		Inspected 96th Field Amb & No 2 Coy Divl Train	
	8.5		Inspected 97th Field Amb.	
	9.5		Inspected 202nd Field Co RE & 21st Inf Bde Hdqrs.	
	10.5		Office & [illegible]	
	11.5		Inspected 98th Field Ambulance.	
	12.5		Inspected D Hdqrs & MMP.	
	13.5		Inspected surplus transport 6th 37th & 9th Divn evacuated [illegible]	
	14.5		Visited MVS	

A5834 Wt. W4973 M687 750,000 8/16 D. D. & L. Ltd. Forms/C.2118/13.

Instructions regarding War Diaries and Intelligence Summaries are contained in F. S. Regs., Part II. and the Staff Manual respectively. Title pages will be prepared in manuscript.

WAR DIARY
or
INTELLIGENCE SUMMARY.
(Erase heading not required.)

Army Form C. 2118.

DDVS 30th Div Vol XXXI

Place	Date 1918	Hour	Summary of Events and Information	Remarks and references to Appendices
BLOXEELE	15.5.		Moved to Eu.	
EU.	16.5		Interviewed Divl Veterinarian 35th American Division & arranged ref offices. Offices arrived	
	17.5.		Instructing Divl Veterinarian ref procedure & returns. Forwarded A 2000 to XIX Corps.	
	18.5		Do ADVS Res Army called.	
	19.5		Acting DDVS XIX Corps called.	
	20.5		Inspected animals issued to 70th (USA) Bde in company with Divl Vet & drew his attention to faults in stable management handling of forage &c.	
	21.5 – 25.5.		Working with Divl Veterinarian regarding Horse management shoeing conditions to be found in the forward area & likely diseases.	
	26.5		Reported DVS took Capt Davis to 14 Vety Hospital to see.	
	27.5		Visited 33rd (USA) Div HdQrs & called on Divisional Veterinarian.	
	28.5		Inspecting units of 35th (USA) Div with Divl Veterinarian	
	29.5		Conference of all V.O.s 35th Div & addressed them regarding work in war zone & forward area with [illegible] of [illegible] & Debility	

A5834 Wt. W4973 M687 750,000 8/16 D. D. & L. Ltd. Forms/C.2118/13.

Instructions regarding War Diaries and Intelligence Summaries are contained in F. S. Regs., Part II. and the Staff Manual respectively. Title pages will be prepared in manuscript.

WAR DIARY
or
INTELLIGENCE SUMMARY.
(Erase heading not required.)

Army Form C. 2118.

DADVS 30th Div Vol XXXI

Place	Date	Hour	Summary of Events and Information	Remarks and references to Appendices
	1918			
El.	30.5		Office work.	
	31.5		Returns in conjunction with Divnl Veterinarian 35. (USA) Divn.	

D H Williamson Major A.V.C.
DADVS 30th Div

A5834 Wt. W4973/M687 750,000 8/16 D. D. & L. Ltd. Forms/C.2118/13.

9

Vol 32

War Diary

-of-

D.A.D.V.S. 30th Divn

for the Month

-of-

June 1918.

Volume XXXII.

Instructions regarding War Diaries and Intelligence Summaries are contained in F. S. Regs., Part II. and the Staff Manual respectively. Title pages will be prepared in manuscript.

WAR DIARY
or
INTELLIGENCE SUMMARY.
(Erase heading not required.)

Army Form C. 2118.

D.A.D.V.S. 30th Division XXXII

Place	Date 1918	Hour	Summary of Events and Information	Remarks and references to Appendices
EU	1.6		Inspecting Units of 35th (U.S.) Div with Divl Veterinarian.	
	2.6.		Visited M.V.S. along with Divl Veterinarian.	
	3.6		Showing Divl Veterinarian 33rd (U.S.) Div and suggesting various matters	
	4.6		Called upon Divl Veterinarian 33rd (U.S.) Divn @ HOPPY.	
	5.6		Inspected ~~D.A.Q~~ — M.M.P.	
	6.6		Visited 96th & 97th Field Ambulance.	
	7.6.		Returns in conjunction with Divl Veterinarian 35th (U.S.A) Div.	
	8.6		Office - Arranging for 33rd U.S. Divn arrival.	
	9.6.		Divl Veterinarian 33rd (U.S.) Divn arrived: EU area.	
	10.6		Visited M.V.S. along with 33rd (U.S.) Divn Divl Veterinarian.	
	11.6		Working with Divl Veterinarian regarding Horse Management; shoeing conditions to be found in forward area & likely Diseases	
	12.6.		Suggestions to Divl Veterinarian for insertion in their Daily Bulletin &c.	
	13.6.		Inspected M.V.S. & Divl Signal Coy.	
	14.6		Instructing Divl Veterinarian 33rd (U.S.) Div ref procedure of returns. Forwarded A 2000 to XIX Corps.	
	15.6		Conference of V.O's of 33rd (U.S.) Div. A.D.V.S. XIX Corps lectured.	
	16.6.		Sick.	
	17.6		Sick: Arranged for Capt Fretwell AVC O.C. 40 M.V.S. to take over my duties.	
	17.6		Major Williamson AVC admitted into No 3 General Hospital.	

A5834 Wt. W4973 M687 750,000 8/16 D. D. & L. Ltd. Forms/C.2118/13.

Instructions regarding War Diaries and Intelligence Summaries are contained in F. S. Regs., Part II. and the Staff Manual respectively. Title pages will be prepared in manuscript.

WAR DIARY
or
INTELLIGENCE SUMMARY.

(Erase heading not required.)

Army Form C. 2118.

DADVS. 30 Divn XXXII

Place	Date	Hour	Summary of Events and Information	Remarks and references to Appendices
EV	17. 6		Arranging for Malleining of 5th Royal Irish Fusiliers who have just joined the Div from Palestine	
	18. 6		In office.	
	19. 6		Visited MVS. & arranged for move of same.	
	20. 6		Moved to RUE	
RUE	21. 6		Office and Returns. Arranging Veterinary Attendance for units of Div left behind in EV area.	
	22. 6		Arranging for Malleining of 2/14, 2/15, 2/16, 2/17, 2/20, 2/23, 2/24 London Regts, 6th Royal Dublin Fusiliers & 5th Royal Inniskilling Fusiliers, just joined Div from Palestine. Furnished record of Mallein Test for 5th Roy Irish Fus: 33 mules + 10 horses all successfully passed the test. / ADVS XIX Corps visited MVS &c.	
	23. 6		Visited No 2 Coy Divl Train + D.H.Q.	
	24. 6		Inspected Divl Signal Coy + RAMC. At MVS. Furnished Record of Mallein Test for London Regts + Irish Regts. 92 Mules + 308 horses all successfully passed the test.	
	25. 6		Inspected 7 London Battalions & 2 Irish Battalions.	
	26. 6		Arranging for move of MVS for 27th Office work	
	27. 6		Moved to EPERLEQUES.	
EPERLEQUES	28 6		Office + Returns: ADVS VII Corps called. Visited MVS &c.	
	29. 6		Visited 97th Field Ambce. MVS &c.	
	30. 6		Visited DHQ, DAMS, Signal Co, 89 Bde HQ, 2/17 London Regt, No 2 Coy Div Train, 202 Field Coy RE. SAA Sect DAC, 2/20 Londons & 21st Inf Bde HQ.	

S Lister
Capt AVC
A/DADVS 30 Division

A5834 Wt. W4973 M687 750,000 8/16 D. D. & L. Ltd. Forms/C.2118/13.

War Diary

-of-

D.A.D.V.S. 38th Divn

-for-

July 1918

Volume XXXIII

16

Instructions regarding War Diaries and Intelligence Summaries are contained in F. S. Regs., Part II. and the Staff Manual respectively. Title pages will be prepared in manuscript.

WAR DIARY
or
INTELLIGENCE SUMMARY.
(Erase heading not required.)

Army Form C. 2118.

VR 33

DADVS 30th Divn Volume XXXIII

Place	Date	Hour	Summary of Events and Information	Remarks and references to Appendices
EPERLECQUES	1. 7.		Line Veterinary Inspection report to G.O.C. Div & ADVS VII Corps. Inspection of 30 Bn ... G ... which joined Division as a new unit from 4 Army on 30/6/18.	
	2. 7.		Sick.	
	3. 7.		Sick. Capt Little AVC took over temporary duty. ~~Inspected~~ 7th Royal Irish Fusiliers and 2 Bn South Lancashire Regt. These 2 Bns just joined Division	
	4. 7.		Arrival of Major J.A. Bosley AVC as DADVS 30th Division: Visited 40 M.V.S.	
	5. 7.		Inspected Divl. Signals. 7/8 Inniskillings. 2nd S. Lancs. Small Arms Sect. 97th Field Amb. Saw A.D.V.S. 2nd Corps.	
	6. 7		Inspected No 2 Coy Divl Train. 2/20 Lond. Rgt. 202 Coy R.E. 2/23 Lond. Rgt 2/24 Lond. Rgt 7th Royal Irish Rgt. No 4 Coy Divl Train	
	7. 7		Inspected with A.D.V.S. 2nd Corps Machine Gun Sect. 2/23 Lond. Rgt. 2/24 Lond. Rgt. 2 Royal Irish Rgt. 97th Field Amb. 2/South Lancs 7/8 Royal Inniskilling Fusiliers. 21st Inf Bde Hd Qrs	
	8. 8		Inspected 40th Mobile ... Sect. Office work.	
	9-8		Moved with Divl Hd Qrs. to Cassel	
	10-8		Inspected 1/6 Cheshires. No 1 Coy Divl Train. H Q 21st Inf Bde & new site of M.V.S. 96, 78 & 98 Field Ambulances	
	11-8		Inspected D.A.C. No 3 Coy Divl Train.	
	12-8		Inspected 148 & 149 Brigades R.F.A. Weekly returns to Corps.	
	13-8		Inspected 2/16 Lond. Rgt. 2/15 Lond. Rgt. 2/14 Lond. Rgt.	
	14-8		Inspected Hd Qr. animals & South Wales Borderers. Sunday.	

Instructions regarding War Diaries and Intelligence Summaries are contained in F. S. Regs., Part II. and the Staff Manual respectively. Title pages will be prepared in manuscript.

WAR DIARY
or
INTELLIGENCE SUMMARY.
(Erase heading not required.)

Army Form C. 2118.

Place	Date	Hour	Summary of Events and Information	Remarks and references to Appendices
CASSEL	15-7.		Inspected 200 Co. R.E. Office work	
	16-7		Inspected 7/8 Inniskillings 17 Lond. Rgt. 2 S. Lancs.	
	17-7		Inspected S/j. Coy HQ Attended conference Divl HQ.	
	18-7		Inspected 77th A.F.A. A. B. C Batteries & A. C.	
	19-7		Office work Weekly returns	
	20-7		Inspected 1/6 Cheshires, 2/23 Lond. Rgt. No H Coy Divl Train	
	21-7.		Sunday. Church. Inspected H.Q. horses.	
	22-7		Attended conference at A.D.V.S' office X Corps	
	23-7		Office work Torrential rain	
	24-7		Inspected 342 Road Construction Coy	
	25-7		Inspected 40 M.V.S with A.D.V.S. X Corps	
	26-7		Inspected 148 Bde R.F.A. with A.D.V.S. X Corps	
	27-7		Inspected Remounts joining Division	
	28-7		Sunday - Church inspected HQ horses.	
	29-7		Inspected M.M.P. Divl. S/j. Coy. 201 Coy R.E.	
	30-7		Inspected 342 Road Construction Coy & 40 M.V.S	
	31-7		Preparing monthly inspection Report & office work	

J. A. Bell[?]
Major AVC

A5834 Wt. W4973 M687 750,000 8/16 D. D. & L. Ltd. Forms/C.2118/13.

War Diary

-of-

D.A.D.V.S.

30th British Division

for Month of

August 1918

24

Army Form C. 2118.

WAR DIARY
or
INTELLIGENCE SUMMARY.
(Erase heading not required.)

Instructions regarding War Diaries and Intelligence Summaries are contained in F. S. Regs., Part II. and the Staff Manual respectively. Title pages will be prepared in manuscript.

DADVS 30 Divn Volume XXXIV

Place	Date	Hour	Summary of Events and Information	Remarks and references to Appendices
TERGEDHEM	1.8.18		Inspected 2/23 Lond. Rgt & H.Q. 21st Inf Bde.	
	2/8/18		Office work, weekly returns & report.	
	3/8/18		Attended French animals injured by bombs, Inspected No 4 Survey Coy.	
	4/8/18		Sunday. Inspected Divl HQ animals	
	5/8/18		Inspected 1/6 Cheshires 200 Coy R.E.	
	6/8/18		Inspected 30th D.A.C.	
	7/8/18		Office work & attending French civilian animals	
	8/8/18		Inspected 90th Inf Bde with ADVS Corps	
	9/8/18		Office work, weekly returns, reports & conference.	
	10/8/18		Proceeded to Corps & took over ADVS X Corps whilst Lieut Col. Knott AVC proceeded on leave	

A5834 Wt. W4973/M687 750,000 8/16 D. D. & L. Ltd. Forms/C.2118/13.

Instructions regarding War Diaries and Intelligence Summaries are contained in F. S. Regs., Part II. and the Staff Manual respectively. Title pages will be prepared in manuscript.

WAR DIARY
or
INTELLIGENCE SUMMARY.
(Erase heading not required.)

Army Form C. 2118.

Place	Date	Hour	Summary of Events and Information	Remarks and references to Appendices
Cassel	10-8-18		Took over duties of D.A.D.V.S: Division moved to TERDEGHEM.	
Terdeghem	11-8-18		Inspected Divisional area for site for Mobile Vety. Section: site of outgoing Division not considered central in this area.	
" " "	12-8-18		Arranged move of M.V.S: M.V.S moved to P.10 d 3.7 (sheet 27).	
" " "	13-8-18		Authority received for daily issue of crushed oats for 100 animals of 90th Infantry Brigade (D.D. of S.T 2nd Army SR 43 10/8/18): French mission arranged for crushing of these oats by Civilian at Bavinchove and S.S.O informed of this arrangement also of issue to units.	
" " "	14-8-18		Inspected 96th and 97th Field Ambulances (R.A.M.C).	
" " "	15-8-18		Suggested various alterations in Mobilization Store Table of M.V.S. Under instruction from 30 Division (Q) selected animals for X Corps Horse Show, at an eliminating Trial of Infantry Brigades Transport.	
" " "	16-8-18		V.Os Conference and A.F.A 2000s: In Office. Submitted names for Course of Instruction in Horse Management, one Officer and two N.C.Os.	

A5834 Wt. W4973/M687 750,000 8/16 D. D. & L. Ltd. Forms/C.2118/13.

Instructions regarding War Diaries and Intelligence Summaries are contained in F. S. Regs., Part II. and the Staff Manual respectively. Title pages will be prepared in manuscript.

WAR DIARY
or
INTELLIGENCE SUMMARY.
(Erase heading not required.)

Army Form C. 2118.

Place	Date	Hour	Summary of Events and Information	Remarks and references to Appendices
Terdeghem	17-8-18		Inspected Hdqts 89 Infantry Brigade and Machine Gun Bn.	
	18-8-18		Inspected Div Hdqts, Div Signals and Hdqts R.A.	
	19-8-18		Inspected No1 Coy 30 Div: Train, 201 Field Coy and 98th Field Amb:	
	20-8-18		Called at 30 D.A.C, 96 Field Ambulance, No1 Coy Div: Train to see selected Brood mares.	
	21-8-18		at Bavinchove: as Divisional Representative at Selection Committee of Brood mares.	
	22-8-18		Rode around Divisional area for a site for a Clipping Depot: Selected site at P.10 b 1.1 (Sheet 27).	
	23-8-18		In Office V.O's conference and A.F.A. 2000: Inspected 30 Remounts on horse lines of Hdqts D.A.C.	
	24-8-18		Inspected 21st Infantry Brigade Hdqts, 1/6 Cheshire Regiment, 9th Royal Irish Regiment and 2/23 London Regiment.	
	25-8-18		Inspected Nos 2, 3, & 4 Coys 30th Divisional Train.	

A5834 Wt. W4973/M687 750,000 8/16 D. D. & L. Ltd. Forms/C.2118/13.

Instructions regarding War Diaries and Intelligence Summaries are contained in F. S. Regs., Part II. and the Staff Manual respectively. Title pages will be prepared in manuscript.

WAR DIARY
or
INTELLIGENCE SUMMARY.
(Erase heading not required.)

Army Form C. 2118.

Place	Date	Hour	Summary of Events and Information	Remarks and references to Appendices
TERGEDHEM.	26/8/18		Inspected 171 Tunneling Coy. Lieut-Col G. P. Knott A.V.C returned from leave	
	27/8/18		Returned to 30th Divl. Hd Qrs. & took over D.A.D.V.S. from Capt. McIntires(?) A.V.C	
	28/8/18		Office work	
	29/8/18		Inspected S. Lancs. 2/17 Lond. Regt. 7/8 Royal Innis. Fusiliers 89th Inf. Bde H.Q. 6th Cheshires. 21st Inf. Bde H.Q. 2/23 Lond. Regt. 90th Inf. Bde H.Q. 2/15 Lond. Regt. 2/14 Lond. Regt	
	30/8/18		Inspected 149 Bde RFA with ADVS Corps	
	31/8/18		Attended X Corps Horse Show	

[illegible signature]
Major

A5834 Wt. W4973/M687 750,000 8/16 D. D. & L. Ltd. Forms/C.2118/13.

19

Vol 35

WAR DIARY.

SEPTEMBER.

1918.

VOL. XXXV.

D.A.D.V.S.

30th BRITISH DIVISION.

Army Form C. 2118.

Instructions regarding War Diaries and Intelligence Summaries are contained in F. S. Regs., Part II. and the Staff Manual respectively. Title pages will be prepared in manuscript.

WAR DIARY
or
INTELLIGENCE SUMMARY.
(Erase heading not required.)

D A D V S 30th Brit: Divn

VOL XXXV

Place	Date	Hour	Summary of Events and Information	Remarks and references to Appendices
LA. MONTAGNE	1/9/18		Divl. Hd Qrs moved to La Montagne.	
	2/9/18		Reconnoitred the new area.	
	3/9/18		Office work & detailing work in new area.	
	4/9/18		Inspected Divl. Ammun. Col. & 200 Coy R.E.	
	5/9/18		Inspected 90th Infantry Brigade	
	6/9/18		Office work, weekly returns & report.	
	7/9/18		Attended conference of A.D.V.S. Corps.	
	8/9/18		Sunday Inspected Divl. Hd. Qrs & Divl Signals	
	9/9/18		Inspected S. A. A. Column.	
	10/9/18		Inspected S. A. A. Column with A.D.V.S. Corps.	
	11/9/18		Pouring rain Office work.	
	12/9/18		Inspected 90th Inf Bde. Hd Qrs.	
	13/9/18		Inspected 2/23 Lond. Rgt 7/Royal Irish & 200 Coy R.E	
	14/9/18		Inspected 202 Coy R.E Office moved in Boeschepbe.	
	15/9/18		Sunday	
	16/9/18		Inspected each individual animal of B 149 Bde RFA owing to case of mange.	
	17/9/18		Inspected 90th Inf Bde with A.D.V.S. Corps.	
	18/9/18		Inspected 97 Field Amb & Machine Gun Bn	

A5834 Wt. W4973 M687 750,000 8/16 D. D. & L. Ltd. Forms/C.2118/13.

Instructions regarding War Diaries and Intelligence Summaries are contained in F. S. Regs., Part II. and the Staff Manual respectively. Title pages will be prepared in manuscript.

WAR DIARY
or
~~INTELLIGENCE SUMMARY.~~

(Erase heading not required.)

Army Form C. 2118.

Place	Date	Hour	Summary of Events and Information	Remarks and references to Appendices
LA MONTAGNE	19/9/18		Inspected 98 Field Amb. & C 149 Bde. RFA	
	20/9/18		Inspected Divl. Train	
	21/9/18		Inspected 6/S.W.B & 201 Coy RE	
	22/9/18		Inspected 89th Inf. Bde	
	23/9/18		Inspected Remounts joining division	
	24/9/18		Divl Hd Qrs moved to St JANS CAPPEL chateau grounds	
	25/9/18		Pouring rain. Visited C 149 Battery & 40th M.V.S.	
	26/9/18		Inspected 21st Infantry Brigade	
	27/9/18		Conference of V.Os. of the division	
	28/9/18		Weekly returns & report. Office work	
	29/9/18		Choosing an advanced site for M.V.S	
	30/9/18		Office work	

J A Bosley Major AVC
DADVS. 30th Divn

A5834 Wt. W4973/M687 750,000 8/16 D. D. & L. Ltd. Forms/C.2118/13.

War Diary

-of-

D. A. D. V. S. 30th Divn

for Month of

October 1918.

Instructions regarding War Diaries and Intelligence Summaries are contained in F. S. Regs., Part II, and the Staff Manual respectively. Title pages will be prepared in manuscript.

WAR DIARY
or
INTELLIGENCE SUMMARY.
(Erase heading not required.)

Army Form C. 2118.

D.A.D.V.S. 30th BRIT. DIVISION.
VOLUME XXXVI.

Vol 37

Place	Date	Hour	Summary of Events and Information	Remarks and references to Appendices
MOUNT NOIR	1.10.18		Divl. H.Q. moved to MOUNT NOIR	
DRANOUTRE	2-10-18		Divl. H.Q. moved to DRANOUTRE	
	3-10-18		Selecting new site for M.V.S.	
	4-10-18		Office work, weekly returns & report	
	5-10-18		Inspected 148 Bde R.F.A	
	6-10-18		Inspected 149 Bde RFA	
	7-10-18		To Corps to see A.D.V.S	
	8-10-18		Office work at M.V.S.	
	9-10-18		Inspected 133 Lab. Coy. 147 Lab. Coy. 93 Lab. Coy	
	10-10-18		Inspected 90th Infantry Bde	
	11-10-18		Office work & weekly returns & report	
	12-10-18		Inspected 21st Inf Bde. 201 Coy R.E.	
	13-10-18		Sunday. Inspected Divl H.Q. animals	
	14-10-18		Inspected 89th Infantry Bde	
	15-10-18		Visited by D.V.S. 2nd Army A.D.V.S. X Corps	
	16-10-18		Office work	
	17-10-18		Inspected 96 Field Ambulance	

A5834 Wt. W4973 M687 750,000 8/16 D. D. & L. Ltd. Forms/C.2118/13.

Instructions regarding War Diaries and Intelligence Summaries are contained in F. S. Regs., Part II. and the Staff Manual respectively. Title pages will be prepared in manuscript.

WAR DIARY
or
INTELLIGENCE SUMMARY.
(Erase heading not required.)

Army Form C. 2118.

Place	Date	Hour	Summary of Events and Information	Remarks and references to Appendices
KORTEWILDE	18.10.18		Divl. H.Q. moved to KORTEWILDE	
	19.10.18		Divl. H.Q. moved to RONCQ	
RONCQ	20.10.18		Office work,	
	21.10.18		Divl. H.Q. moved to AELBEKE	
AELBEKE	22.10.18		Inspected 90th Infantry Bde Took over M.V.S. in addition to present duties	
	23.10.18		Inspected No1 Coy. Divl Train A & B. Coys M. G. B.	
	24.10.18		Inspected No 3 Coy Divl Train 2/15 & 2/16 Lond Rgts. At M. V. S.	
	25.10.18		Weekly returns. Conference of V. Os of the division.	
	26.10.18		Inspected S. A. A Section. No1 & No 2 Sects. D. A. C No 2 Coy. Divl Train. No 4 Coy. Divl Train. 6th South Wales Borderers. 2/23 Lond Rgt.	
	27.10.18		Office work	
	28.10.18		At M. V. S & Divl H.Q.	
	29.10.18		Censoring Board. Inspected No 1 Coy Divl Train. At M. V. S.	
	30.10.18		Inspected 98 Field Amb. At M. V. S.	
	31.10.18		To Field Cashier & X Corps H.Q	

J A Appelby Major AVC
D.A.D.V.S. 30 British Div.

A5834 Wt. W4973 M687 750,000 8/16 D. D. & L. Ltd. Forms/C.2118/13.

War Diary

-of-

D.A.D.V.S.
30th Division

for Month of

November 1918

Volume XXXXII

17

Instructions regarding War Diaries and Intelligence Summaries are contained in F. S. Regs., Part II. and the Staff Manual respectively. Title pages will be prepared in manuscript.

WAR DIARY
or
INTELLIGENCE SUMMARY.
(Erase heading not required.)

Army Form C. 2118.

DADVS 30D

VOLUME XXXVII

38

Place	Date	Hour	Summary of Events and Information	Remarks and references to Appendices
AELBEKE	1.11.18		Inspected No 4 Coy Divl. Train. Attended Board on Shoeing Smiths	
	2.11.18		at M.V.S.	
	3.11.18		Inspected 96 Field Amb.	
	4.11.18		Inspected 38 Lab. Group. 147 Lab. Coy. 70 Lab. Coy. No 1 Coy. Divl Train	
			To Corps to see A.D.V.S.	
	5.11.18		Office work. Inspected Divl. Signals	
	6.11.18		Office work at M.V.S	
	7.11.18		at M.V.S. O.C. M.V.S. Capt Meteries returned from leave.	
	8.11.18		Returns Office work	
	9.11.18		To Corps to see A.D.V.S.	
	10.11.18		Divl. H.Q. moved to Heestert	
	11.11.18		Inspected 202 Coy R.E. 1802 Coy D.A.C. 2/14, 2/15, 2/16 Lond. Regt	
	12.11.18		Inspected 149 Bde R.F.A.	
RENAIX	13.11.18		Divl. H.Q. moved to RENAIX.	
	14.11.18		Office work.	
	15.11.18		Divl. H.Q. moved to MOUSCRON	

A5834 Wt. W4973 M687 750,000 8/16 D. D. & L. Ltd. Forms/C.2118/13.

Instructions regarding War Diaries and Intelligence Summaries are contained in F. S. Regs., Part II. and the Staff Manual respectively. Title pages will be prepared in manuscript.

WAR DIARY
or
INTELLIGENCE SUMMARY.
(Erase heading not required.)

Army Form C. 2118.

Place	Date	Hour	Summary of Events and Information	Remarks and references to Appendices
MOUSCRON	16-11-18		Office work. ~~Reconnaissance~~ reconnoitering new area	
	17-11-18		Sunday. Inspected R. I. R. & Cheshire Regt &	
	18-11-18		Inspected 149 Bde R.F.A.	
	19-11-18		Conference at X Corps.	
	20-11-18		Inspected No 1 Coy Divl. Train. 2/S. Lancs. No 2 Coy Divl Train 30th Bn. M. G. C.	
	21-11-18		Inspected 7/8 Royal Innis. Fus. 2/17 Lond Regt. 6th S. W. B. & 97 Field Amb	
	22-11-18		Conference of V.Os of the Division Inspected M.V.S	
	23-11-18		Inspected 200 Coy R.E. & 89 Inf Bde HQ	
	24-11-18		Inspected Divl Amm Column & S. A. A. Sect.	
	25-11-18		Office work	
	26-11-18			
	27-11-18		Monthly report & meeting of V.Os of Div	
	28-11-18		Inspected 149 Bde R.F.A remounts.	

A5834 Wt. W4973/M687 750,000 8/16 D. D. & L. Ltd. Forms/C.2118/13.

Army Form C. 2118.

Instructions regarding War Diaries and Intelligence Summaries are contained in F. S. Regs., Part II. and the Staff Manual respectively. Title pages will be prepared in manuscript.

WAR DIARY
or
INTELLIGENCE SUMMARY.
(Erase heading not required.)

Place	Date	Hour	Summary of Events and Information	Remarks and references to Appendices
Mouscron	29.11.18		Took over duties of D.A.D.V.S during Leave of absence of Major J. A. Boseley in United Kingdom.	
	30.11.18		Inspected Remounts of 30 D.A.C: Six L D horses from No 1 Section sent to 40 M.V.S for Evacuation.	

H. V. McEtimas
Capt A.V.C
a/D.A.D.V.S
30th British Division

A5834 Wt. W4973/M687 750,000 8/16 D. D. & L. Ltd. Forms/C.2118/13.

War Diary

-of-

D.A.D.V.S.

30th Division

-for-

December 1918

Volume XXXVIII

17

WAR DIARY
or
INTELLIGENCE SUMMARY.
(Erase heading not required.)

Instructions regarding War Diaries and Intelligence Summaries are contained in F. S. Regs., Part II. and the Staff Manual respectively. Title pages will be prepared in manuscript.

Army Form C. 2118.

DADVS 30 D

VOLUME XXXVIII

Vol 39

Place	Date	Hour	Summary of Events and Information	Remarks and references to Appendices
MOUSCRON	1-12-18		Arranging move of Mobile Veterinary Section.	
	2-12-18		Moved with M.V.S to Houplines area.	
RENESCURE	3-12-18		Arrived Ebblinghem Area late at night.	
	4-12-18		Arranging Billets for M.V.S and moved the Section to Renescure.	
	5-12-18		Re-allotting of Veterinary attendance for Units of the Division	
	6-12-18		Officers conference, Returns and Office Work. Veterinary attendance arranged for Corps Units in Divisional Area.	
	7-12-18		Inspected animals at M.V.S before Evacuation to 22 Vety Hospital. Visited 'A' Echelon, Airs reference case of mange in Civilian Horse.	
	8-12-18		Inspected 97th Field Ambulance.	
	9-12-18		Inspected 148 Brigade R.F.A and No 1 Coy Train.	
	10-12-18		Inspected 149 Brigade R.F.A. 3 Field Coys R.E. Animals for Evacuation to 22 Vety Hospital inspected at M.V.S.	
	-12-18		Inspected H.Q. 21st Infantry Brigade, 16 Cheshires and 96 Field Ambulance.	
	12-12-18		Inspected No 4 Coy Train and 7th Royal Irish Regiment.	
	13-12-18		V.O's Conference Returns and Office Work.	

A5834 Wt. W4973 M687 750,000 8/16 D. D. & L. Ltd. Forms/C.2118/13.

Army Form C. 2118.

Instructions regarding War Diaries and Intelligence Summaries are contained in F. S. Regs., Part II. and the Staff Manual respectively. Title pages will be prepared in manuscript.

WAR DIARY
or
INTELLIGENCE SUMMARY.
(Erase heading not required.)

Place	Date	Hour	Summary of Events and Information	Remarks and references to Appendices
Rencurs	14-12-18		Visited M.V.S to inspect animals for Evacuation	
	15-12-18		Inspected 6th S.W. Borders.	
	16-12-18		Inspected No 3 Coy Train and Divisional Signals.	
	17-12-18		At M.V.S. Inspected 2/23 London Regiment.	
	18-12-18		Inspected Divisional H'dqts. H'dqts Divisional Train and M.M.P.	
	19-12-18		Inspected 98th Field Ambulance.	
	20-12-18		V.Os Conference and Returns.	
	21-12-18		Major J. A. Boaley returned from Leave.	
	22-12-18		Major J. A. Boaley on Sick List. continued to act as D.A.D.V.S	
	23-12-18		At M.V.S inspected Horses for Evacuation.	
	24-12-18		Visited C.R.A re arrangements for Xmas Dinner for M.V.S	
	25-12-18		Xmas Day.	
	26-12-18		Inspected 2nd Battalion South Lancs, and H'dqts 89th Infantry Brigade and 7/8 Royal Inniskilling Fusiliers	
	27-12-18		V.Os Conference and Returns.	

A5834 Wt. W4973/M687 750,000 8/16 D. D. & L. Ltd. Forms/C.2118/13.

Army Form C. 2118.

Instructions regarding War Diaries and Intelligence Summaries are contained in F. S. Regs., Part II. and the Staff Manual respectively. Title pages will be prepared in manuscript.

WAR DIARY
or
INTELLIGENCE SUMMARY.
(Erase heading not required.)

Place	Date	Hour	Summary of Events and Information	Remarks and references to Appendices
Renescure	28-12-18		Inspected 30th D.A.C.	
	29-12-18		Inspected 90th Infantry Brigade: Handed over to Major J. A. Bosley.	
			[illegible] Capt R.A.V.C a/D.A.D.V.S	
"	30-12-18		Attended Board on animals of the division 30th British Division for demobilization	
	31-12-18		Inspected 30th Btn. M. G. Corps.	
			J A Bosley Major D.A.D.V.S. 30th Div	

A5834 Wt. W4973 M687 750,000 8/16 D. D. & L. Ltd. Forms/C.2118/13.

24

V8 40 30/

War Diary

-of-

D. A. D. V. S.

30th Division

for month of

January 1919.

Volume XXXIX

Army Form C. 2118.

Instructions regarding War Diaries and Intelligence Summaries are contained in F. S. Regs., Part II. and the Staff Manual respectively. Title pages will be prepared in manuscript.

WAR DIARY
or
INTELLIGENCE SUMMARY.
(Erase heading not required.)

Vol. XXXIX

Place	Date	Hour	Summary of Events and Information	Remarks and references to Appendices
REMESCUPE	1·1·19		Board on animals for demobilization	
"	2 1-19		Attended board on animals for demobilization	
"	3-1-19		" ditto " " " " " "	
"	4-1-19		" ditto " " " " " "	
"	5-1-19		Sunday	
"	6-1-19		Attended board on animals for demobilization	
"	7-1-19		" ditto " " " "	
"	8-1-19		" ditto " " " "	
"	9-1-19		" ditto " " "	
"	10-1-19		Weekly returns & report.	
"	11 1-19		Attended board on animals for demobilization	
"	12-1-19		Sunday	
"	13 1-19		Divl Hd Qrs. moved to LA CAPELLE	
LA CAPELLE	14-1-19		Office work	
	15-1-19		Major G. A. Bosley admitted 14 General Hospital.	

A5834 Wt. W4973 M687 750,000 8/16 D. D. & L. Ltd. Forms/C.2118/13.

Instructions regarding War Diaries and Intelligence Summaries are contained in F. S. Regs., Part II. and the Staff Manual respectively. Title pages will be prepared in manuscript.

WAR DIARY
or
INTELLIGENCE SUMMARY.
(*Erase heading not required.*)

Army Form C. 2118.

Vol XXXIX

Place	Date	Hour	Summary of Events and Information	Remarks and references to Appendices
LACAPELLE	15-1-19 to 23-1-19		Office Work carried out by Clerk and all correspondence submitted to Q Office.	
	24-1-19		Capt. H.V. METIVIER arrived in this area to take over duties of D.A.D.V.S during the absence of Major Beazley R.A. [illegible] in Hospital	
	25-1-19		Inspected the animals of Divisional H.d.q.s.	
	26-1-19		Office Work.	
	27-1-18		Arrangements made with Q and Remount Depot Boulogne for Remount Classification of animals on strength of Div. H.d.q.s and Signal Coy on the 28-1-18.	
	28-1-18		Attended Remount Board.	
	29-1-18		A.D.V.S XIX Corps Called.	
	30-1-18		Office Work.	
	31-1-18		Visited Signal Coys animals and Divisional H.d.q.s.	

4-2-19. H V Metivier Capt R.A.V.C.
a/D.A.D.V.S 30th British Division.

A5834 Wt. W4973 M687 750,000 8/16 D. D. & L. Ltd. Forms/C.2118/13.

War Diary

-of-

D.A.D.V.S.

30 Division

-for-

February 1919

Volume XL

278

Instructions regarding War Diaries and Intelligence Summaries are contained in F. S. Regs., Part II. and the Staff Manual respectively. Title pages will be prepared in manuscript.

WAR DIARY
or
INTELLIGENCE SUMMARY.
(Erase heading not required.)

Army Form C. 2118.

DADVS 30 D

Vol XL

41

Place	Date	Hour	Summary of Events and Information	Remarks and references to Appendices
LACAPELLE	1-2-19		Office Work: arrangements to mallein animals of Divisional Hdqts.	
	2-2-19		Sunday.	
	3-2-19		Z Animals of Div. Hdqts. malleined:	
	4-2-19		Inspected animals of Div. Hdqts. malleined on two occasions between the 24th and 36th hrs after they had been malleined:	
	5-2-19		Completed the malleining of Z animals of Div. Hdqts:	
	6-2-19		Office work: inspected animals malleined on the previous day.	
	7-2-19		Visited Divisional Signal Coy and made arrangements about malleining Z animals on their strength.	
	8-2-19		Office Work.	
	9-2-19		Inspected Div. Hdqts animals: Office work.	

A5834 Wt. W4973 M687 750,000 8/16 D. D. & L. Ltd. Forms/C.2118/13.

Army Form C. 2118.

Instructions regarding War Diaries and Intelligence Summaries are contained in F. S. Regs., Part II. and the Staff Manual respectively. Title pages will be prepared in manuscript.

WAR DIARY
or
INTELLIGENCE SUMMARY.
(Erase heading not required.)

XL

Place	Date	Hour	Summary of Events and Information	Remarks and references to Appendices
La Capelle	10-2-19		Malleined thirty six animals of Div: Hdqts (Signal Coy) at Colembert: Major J. C. Boxley D.A.D.V.S proceeded on 21 days sick leave from 14 General Hospital	
	11-2-19		Completed the malleining of Div: Signal Coy and inspected the animals malleined on the previous day.	
	12-2-19		Inspected the animals malleined on 11/2/19.	
	13-2-19		Office Work.	
	14-2-19		Office Work.	
	15-2-19		Visited D.D.V.S Northern	
	16-2-19		Visited D.D.V.S Northern	
	17-2-19		Inspected animals of Div: Hdqts	
	18-2-19		Visited Divisional Signal Coy:	

A5834 Wt. W4973/M687 750,000 8/16 D. D. & L. Ltd. Forms/C.2118/13.

Instructions regarding War Diaries and Intelligence Summaries are contained in F. S. Regs., Part II. and the Staff Manual respectively. Title pages will be prepared in manuscript.

WAR DIARY
or
INTELLIGENCE SUMMARY.
(Erase heading not required.)

Army Form C. 2118.

XL

Place	Date	Hour	Summary of Events and Information	Remarks and references to Appendices
LACAPELLE	19-2-19		Office Work	
" "	20-2-19		Office Work.	
" "	21-2-19		~~Visited~~ Visited D.D.V.S at Boulogne to arrange about stabling of Div: Hdqts animals in Hardelot Area.	
" " "	22-2-19		Office Work.	
" " "	23-2-19		Office Work (Sunday)	
" " "	24-2-19		Inspected Div. Hdqts animals.	
" " "	25-2-19		Div: Hdqts moved to Condette.	
Condette	26-2-19		Office Work.	
" " "	27-2-19		Inspected animals of Div. Hdqts before they were sent off to No 3 Vety Hospital	
" " "	28-2-19		Office Work.	

2/3/19.

H B Matin[?] Capt
a/D.A.D.V.S
30 Division

A5834 Wt. W4973/M687 750,000 8/16 D. D. & L. Ltd. Forms/C.2118/13.

War Diary

of

D.A.D.V.S. 30th Div.

for month of

March 1919

Volume XLI

Instructions regarding War Diaries and Intelligence Summaries are contained in F. S. Regs., Part II. and the Staff Manual respectively. Title pages will be prepared in manuscript.

WAR DIARY
or
INTELLIGENCE SUMMARY.
(Erase heading not required.)

Army Form C. 2118.

XLI

Place	Date	Hour	Summary of Events and Information	Remarks and references to Appendices
CONDETTE	1-3-19		Routine.	
	2-3-19		Visited DDV.S Northern	
	3-3-19		Routine: Major G.A. Boseley returned from Leave.	
	4-3-19		Handed over to Major G.A. Boseley.	
	5-3-19		Office work. Looking over back work.	
	6-3-19		Routine office work.	
	7-3-19		Capt. Metevier left for No 3. V.E.S.	
	8-3-19		To No 3 Veterinary Hospital to arrange acceptance of cases.	
	9-3-19		Sunday.	
	10-3-19		Visited D.V.S. ~~[illegible]~~ France.	
	11-3-19		Met A.D.V.S. XIX Corps consultation re allotment of duties of V.Os.	
	12-3-19		Routine.	
	13-3-19		To No 13 Veterinary Hospital	
	14-3-19		Routine	
	15-3-19		Inspected H.Q. Signal Coy	

A5834 Wt. W4973 M687 750,000 8/16 D. D. & L. Ltd. Forms/C.2118/13.

27/8

Instructions regarding War Diaries and Intelligence Summaries are contained in F. S. Regs., Part II. and the Staff Manual respectively. Title pages will be prepared in manuscript.

WAR DIARY
or
INTELLIGENCE SUMMARY.
(Erase heading not required.)

DADVS 30 D

Army Form C. 2118.

VR

Place	Date	Hour	Summary of Events and Information	Remarks and references to Appendices
COYDETTE	16-3-19		Sunday	
"	17-3-19		Inspected Nos 3 & 4 Coys. Divl. Train	
"	18-3-19		Inspected H.Q. 30th Bn. M.G.C.	
"	19-3-19		Office work	
"	20-3-19		Routine	
"	21-3-19		To No 3 Convalescent Horse Depot.	
"	22-3-19		Routine.	
"	23-3-19		Sunday	
"	24-3-19		To No 12 Veterinary Hospital	
"	25-3-19		Routine.	
"	26-3-19		Routine. Office work.	
"	27-3-19		Paying [illegible]. Office work	
"	28-3-19.		Inspected South Wales Borderers Transport	
"	29-3-19		Routine. Heavy Snow	
"	30-3-19		Sunday	
"	31-3-19		Office work	

J A Boselly Major
D.A.D.V.S.
30th Div.

A5834 Wt. W4973 M687 750,000 8/16 D. D. & L. Ltd. Forms/C.2118/13.

www.ingramcontent.com/pod-product-compliance
Lightning Source LLC
Chambersburg PA
CBHW081352160426
43192CB00013B/2392
* 9 7 8 1 4 7 4 5 1 5 1 0 8 *